Presented To:

_____

From:

_____

Date:

_____

First
DANCE

DANCE

Venturing Deeper Into a Relationship With God

BRIAN CONNOLLY

DESTINY IMAGE® PUBLISHERS, INC.
P.O. Box 310, Shippensburg, PA 17257-0310

"Promoting Inspired Lives."

This book and all other Destiny Image, Revival Press, MercyPlace, Fresh Bread, Destiny Image Fiction, and Treasure House books are available at Christian bookstores and distributors worldwide.

For a U.S. bookstore nearest you, call 1-800-722-6774
For more information on foreign distributors, call 717-532-3040.
Reach us on the Internet: www.destinyimage.com

ISBN 13 TP: 978-0-7684-3952-6
ISBN 13 Ebook: 978-0-7684-8940-8

For Worldwide Distribution, Printed in the U.S.A.
1 2 3 4 5 6 7 8 9 10 11 / 13 12 11

DEDICATION

This book is dedicated to two people—the first is my daughter, Emma, and any future children that my wife, Nicole, and I would have the blessed privilege to love and nurture. May you, Emma, fall radically in love with Jesus. May you come to know the riches of His grace and His unfailing love for you. May you come to know Him more intimately than I ever could. And may you come to share that love with the world around you. Be His beloved. Be His bride.

Second, I'd like to dedicate this book to a beloved member of Praise Community Church in York, PA—Joyce E. Heltebridle. Joyce passed away suddenly on Saturday, October 2, 2010. She was only 63. Before she died, Joyce was quoted as saying that in the last few months of her life, she truly believed that she was worth the blood of Jesus Christ. Joyce's revelation embodies the purpose of this book.

May we all come to the same conclusion.

ACKNOWLEDGMENTS

I'd like to thank the following people for the following things:

Nicole Connolly

For being the best wife I could ask for. For believing in me and for standing by my side for the last six years. For being an incredible mother to our beautiful Emma. For allowing me to pursue God with all my heart.

Pastor Adam Bower

For being a true brother in Christ. For always being there for me. For encouraging me. For loving me. For being a true answer to prayer.

Pastor Jason Hostetter

For introducing me to the world of the supernatural.

David Daku

For being the very instrument God used to bring inner healing to my life. For being a great listener.

Will Hart

For being a friend. For being a mentor. For always allowing me to ask questions, even if they seemed ridiculous. And for laying your hands on me and saying the word that led me into the greatest God encounter of my life: "Fill."

Ed Garner

For modeling what true faith looks like. For being one of the most passionate men for Jesus and sharing that with me.

Nic and Rachael Billman

For creating music that has enabled me to encounter God through worship in my secret place. For writing music that has put into words what my heart has not been able to express.

Praise Community Church

For providing me the platform through which God has been able to use me. For sending me out to those who are hungry for more.

Endorsements

In his book, *First Dance*, I believe Brian has captured the essence of a love-based relationship with God. He writes with a passion for God out of his own personal experience with God. The blend of theological and psychological realities, when believed and applied through the power of the Holy Spirit, can bring significant change in your life. I encourage you to join Brian in tasting and seeing that the Lord is good.

David B. Daku
Founder of Christian Counseling Services
of Central Pennsylvania

I believe Brian has captured the most powerful weapon in deliverance there is—*love*. Some books talk about it, some teach about it; Brian's book does exactly that and more! If you want to feel love in a tangible way then this book is for you! Get ready to be delivered! Get ready for a love encounter with the Father!

T. Jason Price
Power for Freedom Ministries

Child-like expectations are raised as the reader engages *First Dance*. It returns the reader back to the initial encounter with love, and the reality that there is more for us as the spouse of Christ. We are to know Christ, and through Brian's journey the readers are encouraged to step out in faith into a deeper intimacy with the God who loves them. The Holy Spirit plays a crucial role in our knowing of the Lord; for that closeness that we assumed was in Heaven is in the here and now.

Rev. Adam Bower
Pastor, Praise Community Church
York, Pennsylvania

First Dance offers a challenge to believers and churches alike to experience and connect with the love of God in a deeper way. Connolly calls us as Christians to rediscover love as the central ingredient to our faith, character, fruitfulness, relationships, influence, and growth. Through the story of his own life interacting with Scripture, books, music, and trusted friends and leaders, Connolly offers healing and reminds us that we are worthy of God's love. We as readers discover what can happen when we desire to know God intimately through faith in Jesus Christ and accept the power of God through the presence of the Holy Spirit. We are worth the blood of Christ.

Rev. Dr. B. Michael Brossman
Pastor, Centenary United Methodist Church
Steelton, Pennsylvania

"Where words failed, tears took their place." Brian's striking words offer an invitation into the revelation of the Father's love for all who read this book. As you enter this journey of discovery, you will find that this love offering from God is comforting, satisfying, hope-filled, and a place of safety.

Over the years I have been honored with the privilege of officiating many weddings in a variety of settings, giving me the advantage of seeing the love exchange between a bride and groom. The joy in that moment is beyond words! How much greater is the joy of the heavenly host when a person on earth meets Jesus? As I write, I am overwhelmed with joy as I envision the angelic host responding with excitement as each new person experiences the love of God for the first time. The invitation to believe in your heart and confess with your mouth that Jesus is Lord is like none other! It is in that day that the journey of learning to be a bride begins.

As you read this inspirational exposé of love and relationship, will you open your heart to receive revelation that will set you free? Perhaps you will find what it means to be "born again" in a refreshing new way? A few years ago, God showed me that salvation is not just being saved from hell, but being saved into God's world. Brian has eloquently expressed the nature of this newfound relationship; perhaps today you will experience the same! As you embark on this journey of discovery, invite the Holy Spirit to lead you into truth; truth that will set you free.

Thanks, Brian, for sharing your heart and inviting us into the amazing journey of becoming the Bride of Christ! I will bring to a close my heartfelt confession with praying with you, "Father, I hunger and thirst for You. I want nothing more than to encounter You right now. I pray that You would come and meet me right where I am. I give You full permission to!" Enjoy the journey.

Rob Stoppard
Rob Stoppard Ministries

Brian carries the Father's heart and has powerful, life-changing revelation. This book will inspire, encourage, and give you divine insights on how much you are loved by the Heavenly Father. When you read this book, it will ignite a passion within you to share this amazing love of Jesus Christ with others. Personally knowing Brian, he carries a deep love for all people and desires to see revival in this land.

Ed Garner
Pastor, The Outpouring of Lancaster
Lancaster, PA Life Empowerment, Inc.

Brian has the ability to stir up passion in anyone he meets. His zeal for God is life-giving and contagious. *First Dance* will draw you again into deep places with God and reveal just how impacting and necessary this intimacy truly is for you and for the world. There is a wealth of revelation in this book; however, even the foundational golden nuggets will set you free. This book will cause you to jump into God's passion with both feet.

Will Hart
Hart Ministries

CONTENTS

Part III—Come Up Here, My Beloved, My Bride

FOREWORD

I believe that the role of a worship leader is two-part. The first part is to press in to the heart of the Father and listen for what He is saying. To see where His heart is and to know how to minister to Him just like the Levites did in the Old Testament. Ministering to the Lord is a lost practice in many churches these days. It is more than just singing praise songs in God's direction; it's about touching His heart and listening for His voice. A worship leader must first be in intimacy with God alone before he or she can lead others to that place. It's like the old expression, "you can't give what you don't have," or another way of saying that is, "you can't lead others where you haven't gone yourself." Once you know what is on the Father's heart for a particular service or time, then you know what to sing over the children.

Often as I'm leading worship I'll have a vision of Father God sitting at a piano with a young child sitting next to Him on the piano bench, playing and singing together. This is the second part of a worship leader's role: to help the children respond to the Father.

Zephaniah 3:17 says that the Lord rejoices over us with singing. We love because He first loved us and we sing because He first sang over us. It is true that worship can sometimes be proactive, crying out to God to move or to pour out His spirit; however, worship was designed to be responsive. We respond to the holiness and goodness of God with our song, with our dance, and with our hearts. Our times of worship need to be deeper than just singing songs, even if they are very deep songs. Worship begins in the heart as a passionate response to the song of a loving Father. It's the fusion of hearts as the Father and His children sing together.

The greatest song that the Father ever sang was Jesus. He was a song released on the earth; the heart of the Father sent to sing the beloved back to Him. Jesus is the bridegroom and He sang the song of the bridegroom to draw the bride unto Him. He was the ultimate tuning fork sent to bring the bride and all of creation into perfect harmony with the heart of the Father. We heard His song and we fell in love with Him, even on the cross He sang in sweet surrender. We love because He loves and we sing because He sings; the bridegroom and the bride singing the wedding song together. It's the greatest duet that has ever existed.

First Dance captures this beautiful dynamic between the bridegroom and the bride in a powerful way. It is true worship leadership in the form of a book. As I read through Brian's book I felt myself drawn to inner chambers of the bridegroom. I found myself singing and continually in an attitude of worship as I read through the revelation and insights that God has given Brian. I believe that this book will transform the way that you hear and respond to the Father in worship. My prayer for you is that, as you read through the pages of this book you would be drawn deeper in love with Jesus. He's singing, "Come up here, My beloved My bride." Will you respond?

Nic Billman
Shores of Grace Ministries
A worship and missionary ministry
headquartered in Curitiba, Brazil

THE WEDDING IS READY

I've been best friends with Adam for 11 years. Prior to our meeting at Millersville University in the fall of 1999, I had been asking God to place godly people into my life as I was getting ready to begin the adventure known as the "college life." Little did I know, Adam had also been asking God to send a Christian brother into his life—someone who could fill the void (but never, ever take the place) of the loss of his older brother who passed away a few years prior to our meeting.

It was a match made in Heaven! (Remember, our meeting was the culmination of both our prayers.) We did everything together. We played video games. We watched movies. We exercised. We played on the lacrosse team. We led Bible studies. We even went to seminary together at Asbury Theological Seminary in Wilmore, Kentucky. If you haven't already picked up on it, there was very little that we did apart from one another. Our friendship represented true brotherhood. This truly was a relationship that was wrought together by the intricate workings of God—a God who answered our prayers. This was a David and Jonathan relationship.

On May 29, 2004, I was joined to my beautiful wife, Nicole, on a day that was as beautiful as her. To no one's surprise, I had asked Adam to be my best man. I wanted him to stand side by side with me at the altar while I waited to meet my bride. Because of our history together, it was an obvious decision to not only ask him to be my best man, but to also *invite* him to share in one of the most important days of my life.

On June 19, 2004—approximately three weeks after my wedding day—I stood side by side with Adam once more. Only this time I was his best man.

When you are cherished, appreciated, accepted, and loved by someone, it isn't a shock when you are invited to something as special as his or her wedding day. It isn't a surprise to have the honor of best man or maid of honor bestowed upon you. These are things that make sense to us based on our relationship with that particular person. We can come to expect to be *invited* into knowing and doing life with them.

Why should this be any different between God and man? Surely the God who loved the world so much that He gave His only begotten Son (see John 3:16) must love me more than Adam does. Surely this God cherishes me and accepts me more than my best friend does, right?

Yes. He does.

His love is a radical, all-consuming love that is constantly *inviting* us to go deeper into Him. It's a love that surpasses knowledge (see Eph. 3:19). It's a love that's too great for words. But it is a love that I'm *invited* to know. It's an intimacy that I'm *invited* to possess.

It's a relationship I'm *invited* to enjoy. It's a union I'm *invited* into where I'm the bride and He's the Bridegroom.

RSVP: Accept or Decline?

The choice always has been and always will be ours when it comes to either wanting to know God for the first time or wanting to deepen our relationship with Him after we've said, "Yes." Why? The short and simple answer to that question is this: He's a gentleman. He's never slow about His promises. He's *patient toward us*, not wishing for any of us to perish but for all to come to repentance (see 2 Pet. 3:9). While He remains jealous for His people, He's never forced Himself onto anyone. This is why there were two trees in the garden.

The tree of life and the tree of the knowledge of good and evil were placed in the midst of Adam and Eve's dwelling, the Garden of Eden (see Gen. 2:9). Haven't you ever wondered why God would place a tree in the midst of His prized creation—humanity—bearing fruit that would cause sin to enter the world, if eaten? Although many may already know the answer to this question, I'll seek to answer it anyhow.

My previous pastor, the Rev. Dennis E. Beaver of Evangelical Lutheran Church in Waynesboro, Pennsylvania, answered this inquiry the following way. I remember him explaining to the congregation of First Evangelical Lutheran Church in Mifflinburg, Pennsylvania, that God had to know if those He created were going to choose Him. "It was a choice we had to make," he explained. It was a choice that was going to be made between the trees. The reality of our love for God was before Adam and Eve in the form of those two trees. It's a choice we all have to make every waking moment of our lives. Choose Him? Or choose something else?

Pastor Dennis would often say that God could have created robots to love Him. But nothing could ever compare to a people who would willfully choose to love the Lord their God. And so the invitation is continually placed before us. We're not robots. We have the capacity to choose.

Will you accept or will you decline?

The invitation to know Him does not cease after we pray "the sinner's prayer." It's an invitation for a lifetime. It is an invitation to feast at His banquet table all the days of our lives. We're not waiting to die to experience Him. You can experience Him right now. Tear up that bus ticket whose destination reads "Heaven" and begin to experience eternal life right now.

This is eternal life, that they may know You, the only true God, and Jesus Christ whom You have sent (John 17:3).

Eternal life is "knowing." It's not a destination. It's a relationship.

His hand is constantly stretched forth. Will you dance with Him?

Introduction

FIRST DANCE

The doors swing open wide and I see You waiting for me
at the altar of my destiny.
And roses carpet the ground as I walk down the aisle in rhythm
with Your heartbeat.
There is a banquet table prepared for us.
There is a fresh new wine waiting to be poured out.
So take my hand
(My hand in Yours)
You have my heart
(The one my heart beats for)
And lead this dance
(Two steps to the left)
I'll follow You, I'll follow You
Sing to me
(The words I long to hear)
As you hold me close

(My head against Your heart)
I'm Yours alone
(I'm Yours alone)
You're all I want, You're all I want
The bridegroom comes
(He comes for His bride)
The bridegroom comes
(The pure and spotless bride)
So take My hand
(My hand in yours)
You have My heart
(The one My heart beats for)
I'll lead this dance
(Two steps to the left)
Just follow Me, just follow Me
Sing to Me
(I'll sing the words You long to hear)
As I hold you close
(Hold me closer, closer)
You're My precious bride
(I'm Your precious bride)
And you're all I want, you're all I want.[1]

I love Nic and Rachael Billman's music. The revelation of God's love that is contained in their music is stunning. It draws me deeper into my understanding of His love for me and pulls me deeper into His presence. I often find that the very words they sing become my prayers. There's truly an anointing in their worship that enables the worshiper to connect with the very heart of God. In their music, you can hear the Father singing over you, and in the process you find that you are singing back to Him. There's an exchange that happens between the created and the Creator.

Just recently, I was listening to the song just quoted. When I first heard "First Dance," I was immediately captivated. Very few songs have been able to do this for me. Very rarely will I hear a song with lyrics that cause me to stop doing everything that I'm doing and listen. Such songs actually freeze time and demand the listener's attention.

Now you must understand that I bought this song intentionally. I previewed its 30 second block on iTunes and came to the conclusion that this could be a song I really worship God to—a song that could really help me enter His presence. To be honest, buying "First Dance" wasn't much of a risk because of my love for what God does through Nic and Rachael's music. After all, I have both their albums, *The Invitation* and *The Least of These*.

Shortly after I purchased the song, I burned it to a CD along with some other songs that help me to enter the presence of God. One day at church while I was getting ready to host a ministry training event, I had placed the CD into a CD player and turned it on while I organized the room where the training was to take place. In the midst of the shuffling of chairs and moving tables, I heard God ask me this question while this song was playing: "Brian, do you know why this song is called 'First Dance'?"

"No," I replied.

God then revealed, "It's called 'First Dance' because it's describing the dance you and I will have after we're married."

> *"Let us rejoice and be glad and give the glory to Him, for the marriage*
> *of the Lamb has come and His bride has made herself ready." It was*
> *given to her to clothe herself in fine linen, bright and clean; for the fine*
> *linen is the righteous acts of the saints* (Revelation 19:7-8).

I'm not even sure if "wow" is an adequate response to capture what was revealed to me in that moment. Where words failed, tears took their place.

God revealed an even greater revelation of His love for me through that song. He has a dance reserved particularly for me on that great day of my union to Him, and He has a dance reserved for you, too.

This is why I write this book.

Those who know me closely know that I am passionate about the love of God and awakening people to its reality and encouraging them to go deeper. Many thanks to Nic and Rachael, who've helped me to do just that.

It is my opinion that the Church desperately needs to experience the love of God like never before. For far too long, the Body of Christ has been known for hypocrisy and judgment. It's time that we are known for what Jesus called us to in the first place—love. After all, it is Jesus who said to His disciples that night in the upper room, *"By this all men will know that you are My disciples, if you have love for one another"* (John 13:35). Love is proof of God.

Even Paul himself wrote in First Corinthians 14:1: *"Pursue love."* Why? Because love is the root of fruitful character that must be present with the power of God described in First Corinthians 12 (the gifts of the Spirit). Truly, love itself is the more excellent way (see I Cor. 12:31).

In her book, *No Greater Love*, Mother Theresa says that we should:

> Love each other as God loves each one of you, with an *intense and particular love*. Be kind to each other: It is better to commit faults with gentleness than to work miracles with unkindness.

She also goes on to say this:

> Jesus came into this world for one purpose. He came to give us the good news that God loves us, that God is love, that He loves you, and He loves me. How did Jesus love you and me? By giving His life.[2]

God loves us with a tender love. That is all that Jesus came to teach us—the tender love of God. *"...I have called you by name; you are Mine"* (Isa. 43:1).

The whole Gospel is very, very simple. He's turning and twisting just to get around to one thing—love one another.

This message of love desperately needs to get back into the heart of every believer. It's the key ingredient to healing the sick, relieving people from torment, setting people free, and bringing hope to a lost and dying world.

Love is attractive. Love is contagious. Love is Jesus Christ.

Love is the very heartbeat of Heaven found in the heart of the Father.

Love is the life Jesus lived. Love is the life Jesus tells us to live.

If we lived the life Jesus calls us to live, we would literally change the face of the planet. In the words of Brennan Manning:

> If indeed we lived a life in imitation of Jesus, our witness would be irresistible. If we dared to radically live beyond our self-concern, if we refused to shrink from being vulnerable, if we took nothing but a compassionate attitude toward the world, if we were a counterculture to our nation's lunatic lust for pride of place, power, and possessions, if we preferred to be faithful rather than successful, the walls of indifference to Jesus Christ would crumble.
>
> A handful of us could be ignored by society, but hundreds, thousands, millions of such servants would overwhelm the world. Christians filled with the authenticity, commitment, and generosity of Jesus would be the most spectacular sign of the human race. The call of Jesus is revolutionary. If we implemented it, we would change the world in a few months.[3]

We need to desperately fall in love with Jesus all over again. We need to be consumed by Him. This is your invitation—an invitation to know your God in a very intimate way. This is your invitation to have your life radically transformed by the furious love of your God. May God bring to all who just so happen to be holding this book right now the baptism of fire that John the Baptist said Jesus would bring in Matthew 3:11. It is a true and trustworthy statement: *"Our God is a consuming fire"* (Heb. 12:29). It is my prayer that God burns away within all of us all that is not of Him and fills us with all that is of Him. It is only when we are consumed by Him, when we are obsessed with Him, and when we are filled with Him that we leak Him to the rest of the world.

The world is crying out for love.

God loved the world so much that He gave His one and only Son... (John 3:16 NLT).

God loved the world so much that He gave Him for you and me.

ENDNOTES

1. For information on Nic and Rachael Billman, please visit their website: www.shoresofgrace.com.

2. Mother Theresa, *No Greater Love* (Novato, CA: New World Library, 2001), 20-21.

3. For information on Brennan Manning and his writings, please visit his website: www.brennanmanning.com.

PART I

There's a Calling Out

Chapter 1

WEDDING PLANS

*They heard the sound of the Lord God walking in
the garden in the cool of the day...* (Genesis 3:8).

The Bride

Weddings are absolutely beautiful. Biblically, it's the image of husband and wife that best captures the relationship that is meant to be had between God and His people. In this relationship, we are the bride and Jesus is the Bridegroom. The truth is that some men may not like the idea of being the bride. "That's a weak, feminine image," they may argue.

Not to me.

Truthfully, there is nothing more beautiful than a bride on her wedding day. I can still picture how my wife was adorned on the day we were joined together six years ago. She was radiant. She never looked more stunning. The mere sight of her walking down the aisle brought me to tears. The reality of what that day meant hit me faster and harder in that moment than in one year of preparing to say "yes" to the woman I'd be spending the rest of my days with.

Isn't that an incredible image? "The woman I'd be spending the rest of my days with." I wonder if that's what Jesus had in mind when we read this amazing promise: *"I will never desert you, nor will I ever forsake you"* (Heb. 13:5). That's the kind of statement we want to hear from our God, isn't it? That's the kind of promise we want to anchor our lives in. He stares His Bride in the eyes with His eyes of fiery love and says, "I'll be spending the rest of My days with you."

Being a bride isn't weak. It's strength. Lest we forget, God's Kingdom has the tendency to be a Kingdom of opposites. It's the first that will be last and the last that will be first (see Matt. 20:16). If you want to become great, become the servant of all (see Matt. 20:26). If you want to live, die (see Luke 9:23-24). And in this particular case, if you want to be strong, be joined to the Bridegroom. Be joined to Jesus.

I really enjoy what Dan Mohler of Neck Ministries says about this very idea. He's not afraid to admit that he's dressed for a wedding. He'll openly state that he's a bride and that he looks too good in his dress. It's his robe of righteousness. He'll say that satan can't take it off. God won't take it off. The only one that takes it off, according to Dan, is us. We unzip out of it the moment we mark ourselves unrighteous. We mark ourselves unrighteous when we believe we are unworthy of His love.[1]

I appreciate his security. I appreciate his understanding of his identity. Dan lives within a deep understanding that he is the righteousness of God in Christ. He knows who he is, and it's in the knowing of our being that everything flows out.

It was always meant to be this way.

We were always meant to know who we are in Him and to live in complete intimacy with the Father.

We were always meant to be joined to Him.

We were always meant to wear our wedding gown. Now, thanks to Jesus, "the stained and filthy rags that we once called identity" have been replaced by "garments of white sewn with grace and washed in blood."[2] Do you have your gown on?

In the Beginning

In the beginning, God spoke and things were created (see Gen. 1). That which was not suddenly became that which is. By His decree, things were separated—light was separated from the dark. Dry land was separated from water. God then began to fill the expanses that He created with living things. Birds began to fly in the heavens. Fish filled the deep of the waters. Various animals crawled on the land.

Suddenly, on the sixth day, God does something that was uncharacteristic of His creative genius up to this point. He creates man. But He doesn't create man by speaking. Man did not appear through the phrase, "Let there be...!" No, man was fashioned out of the dust of the ground and the very breath of God. God formed man in the dirt and breathed life into his nostrils (see Gen. 2:7).

Picture this (and I must give Leif Hetland, founder of Global Mission Awareness,[3] the credit for this beautiful image): God blew into the nostrils of Adam, which would have resulted in Adam taking in a deep breath. When we open our mouths wide and pull a heavy amount of air into our lungs, we are able to hear the sound of the rushing wind enter our respiratory system. Leif proposes that Adam breathed in this sound: "Aaaaaab!" and exhaled the remainder of this word for "father" in the Hebrew language: "Baaaaa!"

Abba. Father.

Why does Leif make this assumption? Because the first face that Adam saw was the face of his Father. The first voice he would have heard was the voice of his Father. The first feeling he would have felt would have been love, because God is love (see I John 4:16). The first experience Adam had would have been the experience of being in his Father's presence.

Abba. Father.

This moment in time that Adam experienced with his Father is the picture of the normal Christian life—abiding in the presence of God. The very name "Eden" means "pleasure." Thus, Adam was placed in the pleasure of his Father.

But we know how the story turns out, don't we? We know how temptation came to both Adam and his wife, Eve, through the craftiness of the serpent (see Gen. 3:1-7). Through that one act, the very thing that Adam and Eve possessed with their Father—that relational intimacy they enjoyed together every moment of every day—was suddenly lost.

In their shame, Adam and Eve hid themselves. They were aware of what they did and were instantly in tune with the consequences of their actions (see Gen. 3:7). They became self-focused. They saw they were naked. As a result, they were unable to see God or themselves clearly.

A Shift in Perspective

Now this is what I find to be fascinating. Recently, I was fortunate enough to attend the Power and Love Conference at the Global School of Supernatural Ministry in Mechanicsburg, Pennsylvania and hear Bob Hazlett, founder of Touch of Fire Ministries, speak about this very topic.[4] Bob was quick to point out something that I believe can help change so many Christian mindsets that hold closely the belief that God was incapable of coming into contact with sinful humanity, which is what I was always taught, either directly or indirectly.

It always seemed that what I was presented was this perverted understanding that God was so appalled by my sin that He couldn't come into my presence. I've heard people say that it's because of His holiness that He couldn't come near me—as if I would defile Him in some way. I believe that many who align themselves with this belief point to the fact that Jesus cried out to His Father while the weight of the world's sin was on His shoulders: *"Why have You forsaken Me?"* (Matt. 27:46). The implication is that the Father had forsaken His Son because Jesus was covered in sin.

I don't agree with this belief. I believe that in that moment the Father never left. Rather, because the iniquity of us all fell on Him (see Isa. 53:6), Jesus not only took on our sin, He also took on our shame and guilt, which results in feelings of abandonment. Lest we forget, it was our griefs and our sorrows that that He carried (see Isa. 53:4).

Think of it this way: When a young boy or young girl violates one of their parents' rules and they know that they did, they tend to feel awkward, disconnected from their parents. Why? Because they know they did something wrong. The tendency is to want to hide, either physically or by creating falsehood to cover it up. This was the reaction of Adam and Eve. Unfortunately, fig leaves don't make good hiding places.

We can also look at it this way: If God was incapable of coming near sinful humanity because of His holiness, how could He step down into it in the Person of Jesus? Make no mistake; it's because of His holiness that *we* couldn't come near Him, not the other way around. It's the same principle we find to be in Jesus' words:

> *For everyone who does evil hates the Light, and* **does not come to the** **Light for fear that his deeds will be exposed** (John 3:20).

It's the sinner who is afraid to approach God. Thankfully, it is the kindness of the Lord that leads to repentance (see Rom. 2:4). The only things God has ever been concerned with are the objects of His love and being in relationship with them. Bob Hazlett uses this verse in Genesis 3 to further illustrate this point: *"Then the Lord God called to the man, and said to him, 'Where are you?'"* (Gen. 3:9).

Through this verse, Bob points out that God never said, "Adam, what did you do?" He said, "Where are you?" Bob's point was this: In that very moment, the only thing God was concerned with was restoring Adam back into relationship with Himself. Sadly, so many Christians hear and listen to the voice of the enemy rather than the voice of the Shepherd.

"What did you do?" is a question that has held too many Christians in bondage for far too long. "What did you do?" has been dealt with. It was never God's question, never His voice. "What did you do?" is the voice of condemnation and it belongs to the enemy. That voice, along with the certificate of debt consisting of decrees against us, was nailed to the cross 2,000 years ago (see Col. 2:14). Cursed is everyone who hangs on a tree, for Christ redeemed us from the Law, having become a curse for us (see Gal. 3:13). This implies that all things that seek to separate us from God have been dealt with. They aren't an issue anymore. Jesus stood in our place. He became what I was so I could become what He is—the righteousness of God (see 2 Cor. 5:21). There truly was a great exchange. I got His report card and He got mine.

The question, "What did you do?" no longer gets to have a voice in our lives. Make no mistake, God is asking, "Where are you?" This is the same God who leaves 99 of His sheep to find the one who was lost (see Luke 15:4-7). And it is this same God who has once again made it possible for us to experience Him the same way Adam did in the cool of the garden. Jesus said, *"I am the way…"* (John 14:6). The way to what? The way back to the Father. For no one comes to the Father but through Him (see John 14:6). Through Him we have our access in one Spirit to the Father (see Eph. 2:18).

It is possible, through the grace of God made manifest through Jesus Christ, to once again know the Father in complete intimacy. We are once again *invited* to abide in the presence of God (see John 15:4; I'll say more about this in a later chapter). It is the abiding life that is normal Christianity. It is normal to know God and to hear His voice. It is normal to feel His love. And it is normal in this relationship through Jesus Christ to experience Him in such a way where we are the bride and He is the Bridegroom. In this relationship, He's the male and He is pursuing us.

The Object of His Desire

I am my beloved's, and his desire is for me (Song of Solomon 7:10).

Brennan Manning describes this desire as God's *furious longing* for you and me.[5] God not only loves us; He likes us. And there isn't a single thing He wouldn't do for you or me to see how much He loves us. The sending of His Son was the barometer, the standard measure of how much He was willing to do to have you.

He who did not spare His own Son, but delivered Him over for us all, how will He not also with Him freely give us all things? (Romans 8:32)

Nothing else measures up. Nothing can come close. We were created to be in the pleasure of our Father. You are the object of His desire. All His thoughts are bent toward you (see Ps. 139:17).

Welcome to the normal Christian life.

ENDNOTES

1. For more information on Dan Mohler, please visit his website: www.neckministries.com.

2. Lyrics from the song "The Invitation" by Nic and Rachael Billman, from the album *The Invitation*.

3. For more information on Leif Hetland and his ministry, please visit his websites: www.leifhetland ministries.com and www.globalmissionawareness. com.

4. For more information on Bob Hazlett and his ministry, please visit his website: www.touchoffire.org.

5. Brennan Manning, *The Furious Longing of God* (Ontario, Canada: David C. Cook, 2009), 22.

Chapter 2

THE INVITATION

My beloved responded and said to me, "Arise, my darling, my beautiful one, and come along. For behold, the winter is past, the rain is over and gone. The flowers have already appeared in the land; the time has arrived for pruning the vines, and the voice of the turtledove has been heard in our land. The fig tree has ripened its figs, and the vines in blossom have given forth their fragrance. Arise, my darling, my beautiful one, and come along!" (Song of Solomon 2:10-13)

Tell My People

I love Joyce Meyer.[1] That's just me. Perhaps some of you will read no further after that comment. That's OK. But I've always loved Joyce's ability to "tell it like it is." I also appreciate the hidden treasure she's discovered in God's Kingdom when it comes to understanding how the issues of the heart (i.e. unforgiveness, jealousy, insecurity, etc.) can deeply affect the believer if not exposed and healed. It is my opinion that her insights have caused the gates of hell to tremble, even more so because of her ability to impart to the Body of Christ the need for inner healing and security in our identity in Jesus. There's nothing the devil fears more than a Christian who knows who he or she is!

About a year ago, I either heard or read a quote by Joyce that has stuck with me since I've come across it. I can't let it go! It's become a part of my very being. The reason I am unable to dismiss it is because there is a sobering truth behind it that we all need to understand. Because I am unable to recall where I either heard or read it, I will do my best to paraphrase what she said.

When Joyce was called into the ministry, she asked God this question: "What do You want me to teach?"

He said, "I want you to tell *My people* that I love them."

Joyce replied, "I don't want to do that! They already know John 3:16. I want a deeper revelation to share. They already know that You love them."

God answered (and here is what I want every reader to get), "No they don't. *If they knew that I loved them, they wouldn't do what they do.*"

This quote stuns me on multiple levels. Like I mentioned earlier, it's sobering because it's true and the truth contained in this quote is this: What you do will always reflect what you believe. Hence, God is saying this: "The standard of measure that reveals whether or not someone knows that I love them is their actions. It's their love level."

The one thing that really jumps out at me in the above interchange between Joyce and God is this comment: "I want you to tell *My people*...." God wasn't telling Joyce to tell the unbeliever about His love (although that is mightily important). He was telling her to tell the believer—those whom we would assume already know the love of God.

To Know and Be Known

The reality behind what God was asking Joyce to do is beautifully contained in Paul's writing.

> *For you are all sons of God through faith in Christ Jesus. For all of you who were baptized into Christ have clothed yourselves with Christ. There is neither Jew nor Greek, there is neither slave nor free man, there is neither male nor female; for you are all one in Christ Jesus. And if you belong to Christ, then you are Abraham's descendants, heirs according to promise. Now I say, as long as the heir is a child, he does not differ at all from a slave although he is owner of everything, but he is under guardians and managers until the date set by the father. So also we, while we were children, were held in bondage under the elemental things of the world. But when the fullness of the time came, God sent forth His Son, born of a woman, born under the Law, so that He might redeem those who were under the Law, that we might receive the adoption as sons. Because you are sons, God has sent forth the Spirit of His Son into our hearts, crying, "Abba! Father!" Therefore you are no longer a slave, but a son; and if a son, then an heir through God. However at that time, when you did not*

*know God, you were slaves to those which by nature are no gods. **But
now that you have come to know God, or rather to be known by
God, how is it that you turn back again to the weak and worth-
less elemental things, to which you desire to be enslaved all over
again?*** (Galatians 3:26–4:9)

In this passage, Paul unleashes an incredible truth: We are sons
of God through faith in Christ Jesus. It has nothing to do with our
following of the Law. It has nothing to do with race or ethnicity or
sex (for there is no partiality with God). But it does have to do with
your faith in Christ Jesus. It's the gift of grace!

Paul then goes on to compare the relationship between the Law
and God's people to that of a prince who is preparing to be heir
of his father's kingdom. In the same way that the child is not left
to figure out how to rule the kingdom on his own but has guard-
ians placed over him to teach, equip, and prepare him, the Law was
Israel's teacher or tutor, preparing them for the fullness of the time
when God would send His Son. The hope was that the Law would
reveal man's sinfulness and in the process stir a deep realization on the
inside for man's great need for God. Hence, the Law was to be our
tutor to lead us to Christ so that we might be justified by faith (see
Gal. 3:24). Truly, the Law was to lead us to the One who could save
us, the One who was the propitiation for our sins (see 1 John 2:2).

Through Christ, we've also received the adoption as sons. We
are no longer slaves! We are children of the Most High God! When
we didn't know God, we were slaves to those things or people that
we believed to be God in our lives (those things or people that took
His place).

In the final verse of this passage (verse 9), Paul nails the Galatians with a very loaded, thought-provoking question that gets right to the heart of the matter. You see, the reason why Paul wrote this letter to begin with deals with a poison that was spreading throughout the belief system of the Galatians. Paul preached that salvation was by grace through faith, but some men had disturbed the Galatians understanding by teaching that faith was not enough. You also had to be circumcised and adhere to the works of the Law. This is why Paul asks the question contained in verse 9 (I'll paraphrase): "Now that you've come to know God through your faith in Christ, why is it that you wish to turn back to those things that are incapable of saving you? Why would you want to become a slave to the things you've been freed from?"

The same question could be asked of us who have come to know God's love but manifest lifestyles that are contrary to this supposed understanding. ("If they knew that I loved them, they wouldn't do what they do.") Perhaps the question could be worded this way:

If you have come to know God, or rather to be known by Him, why:

- Do we still do some of things we do?

- Do we still chase acceptance?

- Do we consider our performance?

- Do we worry about what others think?

- Do we push people away when we crave intimacy?

- Are we pushed around by our circumstances?

- Are we afraid?

- Do we continue to return to that same sin again and again and again?

The answer to this question is quite simple. There is still insecurity present in our relationship with God. In other words, there is a deficit in our understanding of who we really are in relation to Him. Unfortunately, Christians are some of the most fear-filled people on the planet today. We say we believe that God loves us, but we still find ourselves enslaved to the same old ways of thinking, the same old patterns of operating.

If Jesus came to set the captives free (see Luke 4:18; Isa. 61:1), then why are so many Christians still in shackles? Why are so many Christians depressed, anxious, angry, jealous, insecure, etc.? Could it be that so many don't believe? Could it be that so many don't know Him in a way that truly liberates them? I'll address what I believe to be the answers to these questions in the next two chapters.

ENDNOTE

1. For more information on Joyce Meyer, visit her website: www.joycemeyer.org.

Chapter 3

DINNER OPTIONS: FISH OR CHICKEN?

O taste and see that the Lord is good... (Psalm 34:8).

Come Out, Come Out, Wherever You Are

One of my favorite games to play as a young boy was "Hide and Seek." To be honest, I was quite good at it. As I got older, "Hide and Seek" evolved to more age appropriate games such as "Flashlight Tag," "Kick the Can," and "Ghosts in the Graveyard." Although these games weren't as elementary in play as "Hide and Seek," they still contained the element of hiding.

I've always been good at hiding. Even in my adult years (as silly as this sounds), I still consider myself to be good at hiding. I had to be as a youth pastor for four and a half years with some of the games we played as a youth group!

The truth is, many of us are good at hiding, but not in the sense that I'm describing above. Unfortunately, many of us are good at hiding from love—in particular, God's love. Sadly, we do this without even realizing it and it's rooted in what we believe about God and ourselves. We'll talk more about this in the next chapter.

Please understand this—the problem is never on His end. God wants to be known. He's always wanted to be known. This idea is greatly illustrated in Hebrews.

> *God, after He spoke long ago to the fathers in the prophets in many portions and in many ways, in these last days has spoken to us in His Son, whom He appointed heir of all things, through whom also He made the world. And He is the radiance of His glory and **the exact representation of His nature**...* (Hebrews 1:1-3).

The writer of this passage is essentially saying this: Whatever you know about or see to be in Jesus is exactly who the Father is. So when you read Jesus' response toward the woman who was caught in adultery and who was laid at His feet in John 8, we are essentially reading the Father's response:

> *Straightening up, Jesus said to her, "Woman, where are they? Did no one condemn you?" She said, "No one, Lord." And Jesus said, "**I do not condemn you, either. Go. From now on sin no more**"* (John 8:10-11).

Jesus' very words were the Father's words. He only ever did what He saw His Father doing (see John 5:19). If Jesus healed, it was what the Father was doing and wants to do. If Jesus cast out a demon, it was what the Father was doing and wants to do. If Jesus forgave someone, it was the Father forgiving. You get the picture.

Jesus Himself put it this way: "If you've seen Me, you've seen the Father" (see John 14:9). Paul, in his letter to the Colossians, says this: *"He [Jesus] is the image of the invisible God"* (Col. 1:15).

When it comes to knowing God—what He is like, the things He does, and what His will is—we are without excuse. He has made Himself *perfectly* known through His Son, Jesus. God is not playing "Hide and Seek."

Unfortunately, it is possible to *believe in Him* but not *know Him.* Believing and knowing are two separate things. Similarly, knowing about someone is much different than truly knowing them through a relationship, which is what God has invited us into through His Son.

Recently, God had shown to me in Genesis what His desire is in our relationship with Him. The writer of this verse writes: *"And the man and his wife were both naked and were not ashamed"* (Gen. 2:25).

This is pure, unadulterated intimacy. This is His plan for a relationship with us. We are the bride and He is the Bridegroom. We are to become one. There's to be complete self-disclosure from both parties.

Now let's go back to the idea of "knowing about" versus "knowing through relationship." It's possible for me to know about famous basketball legend, Michael Jordan, without ever knowing him through relationship. Unfortunately, all I could tell you about him is facts: He played for the Chicago Bulls. He wore number 23.

He was approximately 6 feet 7 inches tall. He played as a shooting guard. He won multiple championships, etc., etc., etc.

When the best we can do is accumulate facts about someone without knowing them through a relationship, we are left with religion. It's possible to know everything there is to know about someone—study their life, observe them, and even search for them—and yet not *truly know them*. The Pharisees did this. They searched the Scriptures believing that in them was eternal life, but Jesus tells them that the Scriptures testify about Him (see John 5:39). In other words, the very Word they were studying was to lead them to encounter Jesus—to recognize the very Word that became flesh standing before them.

Similarly, you could tell me that you're married, but I would know nothing about the relationship you have with your spouse. Telling someone you're married does not reveal the intricate dynamics of your relationship. We cannot know how you handle arguments, what life is like behind closed doors, whether or not you spend quality time together, etc.

To say that you are a believer, like marriage, does not reveal whether or not you have a relationship with God. It does not illustrate whether or not you *truly know Him*. This was my story for the last 30 years.

I Didn't See That One Coming

My first real, true experience with God came at the expense of a drug-ridden life that had nowhere to go—that actually resulted in a near overdose experience with crack cocaine. I was 19 years old, addicted to things that were slowly taking my life away. I had always believed in God. I even would have told you through my worst times that Jesus Christ was my Lord and Savior, but there was no evidence, no fruit in my life to back such a statement up.

It was in my living room at the age of 19 that God manifested Himself to me through a video my mom had popped in the VCR. On the television was a man who was singing about how the blood of Jesus covered him. I can still see this man's face today as if this happened yesterday.

What happened next, I cannot explain. Tears began to stream down my face and the realization that I was forgiven of my sins hit me like a ton of bricks. In that moment, I was instantly set free of my addictions. Drug abuse. Cigarette smoking. All of it was swept away in the waters of His grace. It was this very encounter that catapulted me into desperately wanting to know this amazing God and stirred a passion within my soul to read His Word.

God delivered me from bondage. I was a slave to my sin, caught in the violent cycle of addiction. Literally, in a matter of seconds, God set free. But the roots that produced the fruit of my addictions had not yet been severed. It is indeed God's plan for all of us to be uprooted from the issues of our heart and be replanted, rooted and grounded in His love and grace (see Col. 2:7).

Because the issues that produced the fruit of my sinful behaviors hadn't been dealt with, I found myself a few years ago in a really bad place.

Up until this point, I was serving in ministry as youth pastor at First Evangelical Lutheran Church in Mifflinburg, Pennsylvania. It was the summer of 2008 and I was three years into my ministry. At the ripe ole age of 29, I could sense that something was wrong on the inside of me. I began to realize the depths of how insecure I felt and my desperate need for approval. I noticed that I was losing joy and becoming depressed. Ministry didn't excite me. Quite honestly, it began to frighten me. I knew I needed help. I knew I needed to talk to someone. I felt like I was in a tangled web that I couldn't get out of. Here I am, a graduate from Asbury Theological Seminary with an MA in Counseling, and I couldn't help myself.

After discussing my situation with a friend at the church who I knew was seeing a Christian counselor and who I knew was experiencing great breakthrough in her sessions, I decided it was time that I do the same.

I myself experienced breakthrough during my first session. My counselor, David Daku, founder of Christian Counseling Services of Central PA, explained to me that I had a deep rooted fear of rejection that stemmed from painful childhood experiences. This very statement resulted in tear-stained cheeks. It was something I had always known, especially if I look back at the patterns by which I related to others. But something happened when David spoke it out loud. It became real. I couldn't hide from it. It was exposed. And it explained so much. It revealed so much of why I did what I was doing. It explained my need for approval. And it explained why I was in the situation I found myself in. The lights came on. I was on the path of healing. I was on the path of finding the truth that was going to set me free (see John 8:32).

All my life I experienced abandonment and rejection. This resulted in a faulty belief system within me that said I wasn't worthy, people will leave you, and you have to perform. David helped me to see that because of these beliefs, I pushed people away. It was my way of controlling the environment around me. If I could keep you away, you couldn't hurt me. It was my defense mechanism.

David helped me to see that the very thing I craved, I hid from. I even began to realize that I was hiding from the love of God. Perhaps I believed that He would hurt me like everyone else. Perhaps I believed that deep down I wasn't worthy of His love. If I was worthy of love, then why would people hurt me and reject me? Sadly enough, many people will take their painful experiences and transfer them onto God (whether they are aware of it or not), believing Him to be the same as everyone else.

Because I had closed myself off from receiving His love and allowing myself to be known by Him, I was dying inside. Whenever a person does not feel good about themselves inwardly, they will go outside of themselves to get those good feelings. They will turn to drugs, sex, fame, fortune, food, alcohol, etc. This was me.

During one of my sessions with David, he said something that has remained embedded in my memory since the day I heard it. He said that *the essence of sin is the disbelief that God is good*. In other words, we turn to the things that are harmful because *we don't really know who God is*. We don't believe He is good and so we often turn to instant gratification. We've allowed our experiences in life to dictate what His character is like rather than allowing the truth of His Word to reveal who He is to us.

Knowing and Being Known

Knowing is everything. Being known by Him and knowing Him is absolutely critical in this relationship (relationships always take two people). Jesus Himself said that eternal life was knowing Him and the Father (see John 17:3). Eternal life is not a destination. It's found in a living, breathing relationship with the Father.

The importance of allowing ourselves to be known by God is found in the sobering reality of Jesus' commentary in Matthew 7. Jesus says this:

> *Not everyone who says to Me, "Lord, Lord," will enter the kingdom of heaven, but he who does the will of My Father who is in heaven will enter. Many will say to Me on that day, "Lord, Lord, did we not prophesy in Your name, and in Your name cast out demons, and in Your name perform many miracles?" And then I will declare to them,* **"I never knew you; depart from Me,** *you who practice lawlessness"* (Matthew 7:21-23).

I know that many people over the years have discussed this particular passage of Scripture, coming up with ideas of what Jesus was talking about. But I believe that these very words capture the truth that it is possible to *believe in Him* but not *fully know Him* or allow yourself to be known by Him. His name has power. This is why these people were able to prophesy in His name and cast out demons and perform many miracles. But there is no evidence of a relationship present.

Jesus words are stunning: *"I never knew you."* Let's face it, if these people were walking in relationship with God, they wouldn't be practicing lawlessness. The fruit of their relationship would be apparent. Jesus would have known them.

One of the most difficult things I had to admit to myself during my process of healing was that my ministry was more about me than anything else. I came to the conclusion that I was more interested in how the students made me feel than how I made them feel. My ministry was feeding me, not my relationship with God. I believe that this is what we find to be present with the men Jesus tells to depart from Him. Could it be that ministries that are done in our name and not His are truly deeds of lawlessness?

Truth Encounters

I will forever be indebted to my counselor, David, for how he helped me to see the truth about who I am in Christ and the love that God has for me. One of the things that David would often say during our sessions is the very verse found at the beginning of this chapter: *"O taste and see that the Lord is good"* (Ps. 34:8). David would continually invite me to feast at the Lord's table to taste of His great love for me.

Time and time again, David led me into truth encounters that helped to set me free. One of the things I learned to meditate on was this: Because of Christ and His redemption, I am completely forgiven and fully pleasing to God. I am totally accepted by God (see Rom. 5:1; Col. 1:22).

It is in these truth encounters of God's love for you and me that we come to know Him and ourselves. It's here that we are set free and are invited into a greater intimacy with Him.

A.W. Tozer says this about this very real fact:

> The Bible assumes as a self-evident fact that men can know God with at least the same degree of immediacy as they know any other person or thing that comes within the field of their experience. The same terms are used to express the knowledge of God as are used to express knowledge of physical things. *"O **taste** and **see** that the Lord is good"* (Psalm 34:8). *"All thy garments*

smell *of myrrh, and aloes, and cassia, out of the ivory palaces"* (45:8). *"My **sheep** hear My voice"* (John 10:27). *"Blessed are the pure in heart: for they shall **see** God"* (Matthew 5:8). These are but four of countless such passages from the Word of God. And more important than any proof text is the fact that the whole import of Scripture is toward this belief.[1]

What can all this mean except that we can know God as certainly as we know material things through our familiar five senses?

We are *invited* to know Him in every way imaginable. We are invited to hear Him, see Him, taste Him, and smell Him. We must begin to train our senses to pick up on these realities that Tozer speaks of (see Heb. 5:14).

God wants to be known. Just as I mentioned earlier in this chapter, we are without excuse. In the next two chapters, we will explore in greater detail the reasons why people hide from God and the condition that I believe the church is in at large.

ENDNOTE

1. A.W. Tozer, *The Pursuit of God* (Camp Hill, PA: Wing Spread, 2006), 48-49.

Chapter 4

THE BRIDE'S REJECTION; THE BRIDEGROOM'S BROKEN HEART

What a man desires is unfailing love...
(Proverbs 19:22 NIV).

Hidden Treasure

Approximately three years ago, God had given me a revelation unlike any that I had received prior and it still rocks me to the core today. Receiving it was cathartic. It was one of those "aha" moments. It was a revelation concerning the state of both Christians and non-Christians alike. To be honest, it was a revelation about where I found myself to be prior to my entering counseling. I find that's how God often works in my life. I find that I'm often teaching to others what He's teaching me in the moment.

What I find to be so fascinating is the actual avenue by which God opened my eyes to this new understanding into my life and the lives of others. Now of course we understand that God speaks and that He can use various means to get our attention. I guess I just wasn't expecting to receive what I did through this particular song that I just so happened to be listening to one day on the radio.

Now for some of you reading this, what I'm about to say next may come as a shocker. The song that God used to speak to me wasn't a contemporary Christian song. Rather, it was a song found on secular radio; a song performed by Leona Lewis called "Bleeding Love."[1]

Revelation Revealed

What I'd like to do now is take you on a journey through the lyrics of this song and share with you the revelation God had given me through it. Let's start with the first two lines of this hidden treasure:

> *"Closed off from love I didn't need the pain.*
> *Once or twice was enough and it was all in vain."*

Through these words, God had shown me that this was not only where I found myself prior to entering counseling, it is also where the majority of the world finds itself today. Through these two lines, Leona is saying this: "I've been hurt way too many times by people (more than likely by men in the context of the song) and I've had enough. I don't want to be hurt again. I should have learned my lesson the first time if not the second. I'm putting my walls up." Truly, these two lines of this song can be summed up this way: "I am no longer allowing myself to be loved or to love someone else. The risk is too great and the pain is unbearable."

A person's hurt or pain can have multiple sources. Perhaps you were abused as a child either physically, emotionally, or sexually. Perhaps one or both of your parents weren't present due to divorce or work or an addiction. In some cases, both parents are present, but their minds are elsewhere or one parent is having to take care of the other because one parent is swallowed up by an addiction (i.e. alcoholism). Whatever the source of the pain within a person, the response is often the same: I'll protect myself by walling myself in. You can't hurt me if I don't let you get to me in the first place.

This is exactly what I did for 29 years of my life. Because of the depths of my pain, I built walls (without even knowing) it that imprisoned me from the very thing I wanted the most but feared the most—love. I feared it because it let me down in the form of many people.

You see, when someone is hurt, let down, abused, neglected, or abandoned, the only means of survival from such trauma is to protect yourself from the emotional weight of those negative experiences. Unfortunately, we close ourselves off from the very thing that we need most and will heal those damaged emotions. This is what Leona is declaring through the lyrics to this song. This is what so many people wind up doing without their actions ever registering on their own radar.

Fortifying your heart with walls is an unconscious action—an action that goes unnoticed from our conscious awareness. We learn how to survive at a very early age as children, and these very survival methods can come along with us and be practiced well into our adult years, if not for the rest of our lives. The problem is that when damaged emotions lie underneath the surface for too long, they can spoil the inside of a person, resulting in bad fruit (i.e. insecurity, jealousy, mistrust, anger, unforgiveness, etc.). It's no different from leftover dinners that have survived in the refrigerator long past their expiration date. Both illustrations have one thing in common—they can begin to stink!

The next line within the song is this:

"Time starts to pass; before you know it you're frozen."

We can actually waste our entire lives by closing ourselves off to the idea of being loved and risking it to love others. We become frozen because we shelter ourselves from the very thing we need most and were created for. It's this very idea that leads me to the second to last line in the verse and is by far my favorite. Leona sings:

"My heart's crippled by the vein that I keep on closing."

This is my favorite line because it's metaphorical. It's also my favorite because the greatness of the revelation contained within this song comes largely from those 11 words. Leona is saying that her heart is in pain and it is no longer functioning; it's paralyzed. The reason why it's not functioning is because she's collapsed the vein.

Physically speaking, veins carry blood to the heart. They provide the heart with what it needs to live. Blood is the life source within the human body. Spiritually speaking, love is our life source. Jesus Himself said that we are to abide in His love because apart from Him *we can do nothing* (see John 15:4-5). In Him we live and move and exist (see Acts 17:28).

In this song, the reason why Leona's heart is crippled is because she's not allowing love to be pumped to her heart. Similarly, our hearts (our inner man) will not function properly if we close ourselves off from the love of God. Indeed, the truth is this: We were created to receive love and give it away.

In the book of Genesis alone, we quickly learn three key things about God:

1. He's a Creator.

2. He's loving.

3. He's holy.

What do you do if you're someone who is full of love and you like to create? You create objects to be loved. Hence, God creates Adam. But God later saw that it wasn't good for Adam to be alone. He needed a helper. He needed someone he could share the love he was receiving from God with. Thus, God creates Eve (see Gen. 2:18). In this beautiful account, we see the two great commandments at work: Man loving God and others by receiving the love of God (see Matt. 22:37-39; I John 4:19).

Unfortunately, our pain not only closes the veins that carry blood to our heart, it can also close our arteries that carry the blood away from our heart too. *We cannot give love if we cannot receive love.*

But there's hope, which brings us to the chorus of the song:

> *"You cut me open and I keep bleeding, keep, keep bleeding love,*
> *I keep bleeding, I keep, keep bleeding love,*
> *Keep bleeding, keep, keep bleeding love,*
> *You cut me open...."*

Prior to being cut open, there was a buildup of love that was ramming up against the walls of Leona's heart. Because of her decision to protect herself from being hurt again, love had nowhere to go. But as the song would have it, she meets a man who has caused her to be open again to the very idea of love. As a result, she's cut open and the blockage of love finally has a place to go. Although this sounds like a happy, mushy ending to a sappy romance movie, there is only one person who is capable of re-opening our veins and removing the blockage that prevents us from receiving and giving love—Jesus Christ.

Whereas Leona found herself cut open by the love this man supposedly had for her, Jesus found Himself cut open for the love He had for us.

> *But He was **pierced through** for our transgressions, He was crushed for our iniquities; the chastening for our well-being fell upon Him, and by His **scourging** we are healed* (Isaiah 53:5).

> *Greater love has no one than this, that one lay down his life for his friends* (John 15:13).

The Revelation Continues

I will never forget what God said to me when I made the decision to go to counseling and deal with my damaged emotions. He took me to Philippians:

> *Now I want you to know, brethren, that my circumstances have turned out for the greater progress of the gospel, so that my imprisonment in the cause of Christ has become well known throughout the whole praetorian guard and to everyone else, and that most of the brethren, trusting in the*

Lord because of my imprisonment, have far more courage to speak the word of God without fear (Philippians 1:12-14).

Although Paul is referring to his current circumstance of literal imprisonment in the physical sense, God was showing me that He was going to heal me of my pain that imprisoned me for so long. As a result, others would have the courage to seek their own healing and have the courage to speak about how God healed them without fear. Truly, it was in my own process of healing and being awakened to the great love that God had for me that I began to understand why people do what they do. Everyone has a story. Not only that, He opened my eyes to the abundance of pain within individuals—pain that has caused people to not believe in God or trust that He is good.

The truth is that a person doesn't decide that God exists or doesn't exist with their mind. They make this decision within their heart. Psalm 14:1 says: *"The fool has said in his heart, 'There is no God.'"*

Unbelief is a posture of the heart—the wounded heart that has been hurt, abused, lied to, rejected, abandoned, and neglected. First John 4:16 says that God is love. Perhaps when people say that they don't believe in God they are saying that they don't believe in love. To not believe in one is to not believe in the other as well.

There's no question that how we are treated by one another affects how we see God. This is why Jesus said that all men will know that we are His disciples if we love one another (see John 13:35). It's difficult when those who are supposed to love us most have hurt us the most (i.e. our parents, teachers, coaches, friends, etc.). It's our experiences with pain that can actually begin to shape our worldviews of God, ourselves, and others. We can readily conclude that God and everyone else will treat us in a way that others have, which resulted in deep wounds. We can also conclude that maybe we deserved to be treated that way. Perhaps all we deserve is to be hurt over and over again.

In A.W. Tozer's book, *Knowledge of the Holy*, he makes this stunning remark:

> What comes into our minds when we think about God is the most important thing about us.[2]

In other words, the most important thing about you and I is what we think about when we think about God. Why? Because whatever I believe about Him will determine how I will relate to Him. If I allow my past experiences of pain and how people have treated me to explain Him, I will push Him away. I will hide from Him. I will resist His love. All the while it's possible for me to do this under the guise that I believe He loves me and I love Him. I could do it because I know all the right answers. I could do it and not even be aware *that* I'm doing it.

What will often wind up happening is this. We will draw a line in the sand based on how people have treated us and we'll say, "God must be like _____."

In his book, *Soul Cravings*, author Raphael Erwin McManus adds to the argument this way:

> The dark side of human community can lead us to give up on God or to recognize He is exactly what we need most.[3]

Sadly, we all too often allow our circumstances and experiences to communicate what God is like rather than allowing the truth of His Word to declare His nature—love.

The Broken Heart of God

I believe it's easy to resist the idea that God loves you when your life experiences contradict the way He loves. I believe it's easy to have the wrong picture of God for the same reason. I also believe that's why God sent Jesus—so we wouldn't have the wrong picture: "If you've seen Me, you've seen the Father" (see John 14:9). Unfortunately, some people are still unable to see the true nature of the Father even when it's standing right in front of them (see Philip's comment in John 14:8).

All God has ever wanted was for us to truly know Him and in the process have a relationship with Him. I find that the heart of God breaks when we are unwilling to believe that He really is who He says He is and trust Him enough to pursue Him in the same way He pursues us. This is captured in no greater detail than when the heart of God laments over the rejection of His people, Israel. Jesus says this:

> *Jerusalem, Jerusalem, who kills the prophets and stones those who are sent to her! How often I wanted to gather your children together, the way a hen gathers her chicks under her wings, and you were unwilling* (Matthew 23:37).

The very people whom God came to save did not receive Him (see John 1:11). So many people today, because of painful experiences, are following the footsteps of Israel—they are rejecting God, and it's breaking the heart of the Bridegroom. He longs to gather us together under the wings of His love and heal every aspect of our lives.

In her song, "My Love Hasn't Grown Cold," Christian artist and singer Bethany Dillon captures the beautiful, loving heart of God that so desperately wants to gather us under His wings and wants us to know Him and His amazing love. Her very lyrics helped me on my own path of healing and being able to trust God with my heart. Indeed, Bethany's words paint a breathtaking image of God that leads the listener, or hopefully in this case the reader, into an encounter with God's supernatural ability to bind up the brokenhearted (see Isa. 61:1). May her lyrics bring you into an encounter that exposes you to the love of God in a brand new way. Bethany writes:

> *You, you shake your head.*
> *What is so hard to believe?*
> *When you are in your bed*
> *I sing over you the sweetest things.*
>
> *Because oh, my love does not tire.*
> *I'm awake when the moon is full,*
> *And I know the times when you feel lost*
> *And you just aren't sure.*
>
> *And lo and behold,*
> *My love hasn't grown cold*
> *For you.*
>
> *You could steal away in the middle of the night*
> *And hide in the light of day*
> *While you cloak yourself in the darkest lies,*
>
> *But oh my love, it swims in the deepest oceans of fear*
> *And as soon as you lower your head*
> *I, I am here.*

Lo and behold,
My love hasn't grown cold
For you.

If only you could see
How heaven stills when you speak.
I know all your days
And I have wrapped you in mystery.

And oh, my love for you
Is as wide as the galaxies.
Just hold out your hand and close your eyes
And come be with me.

Lo and behold,
My love hasn't grown cold
For you.[4]

Oh, if we could only see the very fact that God's love for us is as wide as the galaxies. If we could only find the courage to truly trust His love and grab hold of His hand.

His love has never grown cold. Not once. Not even in the worst of circumstances. Not even when we were treated harshly. Not even when we did that one thing we wish we could undo. No, His love has never grown cold. It burns for you. And I pray, in the same way that Paul prayed, that:

> *...the God of our Lord Jesus Christ, the Father of glory, may **give to you a spirit of wisdom and of revelation in the knowledge of Him*** (Ephesians 1:17).

And that:

> . . .*Christ may dwell in your hearts through faith; and that you, **being rooted and grounded in love**, may be able to comprehend with all the saints **what is the breadth and length and height and depth, and to know the love of Christ which surpasses knowledge, that you may be filled up to all the fullness of God*** (Ephesians 3:17-19).

The Two Sides of the Coin

I've found that pain can do one of two things—drive a wedge between us and God or lead us to Him. Pain can be the very catalyst that leads people to ask the age-old question: "If God loved me, then why did He let this happen?" or it can be the very thing that causes you to collapse in the arms of your Father. The truth is you were created for love. Anything that is keeping you from being open to the love of God is a tool of the enemy to keep you from knowing Him. We must speak that bluntly.

McManus says it brilliantly:

> We are created to know God and to know love. It is love that moves God toward us and love that pulls us toward Him. Follow love and it will guide you to God. From the very beginning you were made for love. It may be hard to accept, but you are the object of God's love. You were created out of love by Him, and though you may not yet realize it, your soul longs to know this love.[5]

Do not let your past determine who you are today or what you will believe. Do not let painful experiences separate you from the

One who can heal and redeem them. It is He and He alone who gives beauty for ashes and causes all things to work together for good for those who love Him (see Isa. 61:3; Rom. 8:28). There is no wound that He cannot heal, no pain that He cannot remove, and no bad situation that He cannot make good.

Do You Want to Get Well?

In the year's time I spent in counseling, my counselor David and I spent a lot of time examining my past. We talked about the effects my parents' divorce had on me as well as other mistreatments that I had accumulated throughout my life. We discussed my fear of rejection, my need for approval, and my self-loathing. The truth is, I didn't like myself very much and I didn't think I was worth very much. This is what my experiences communicated to me and I internalized them. But I was tired of the havoc they were wreaking in my relationships with others, especially my relationship with God. I was fed up with the bad fruit in my life.

One day in session, David dropped this bomb on me. He talked about the man who had been ill for 38 years in John 5. This man waited for the angel of God to come and stir the waters of the pool called Bethesda.

> For an angel of the Lord went down at certain seasons into the pool and stirred up the water; whoever then first, after the stirring up of the water, stepped in was made well from whatever disease with which he was afflicted (John 5:4).

Sadly, the man in the story couldn't get in. Someone always beat him to the punch and no one ever helped him.

When Jesus saw the man in the condition he was in, He asked him a very simple question: *"Do you wish to get well?"* (John 5:6). It is here that David pointed out to me that Jesus walks by us every single day asking the very same question: "Do you wish to get well?"

Who wouldn't want to get well?

The truth is there are some people who wish to remain the way they are. To get well requires responsibility. To get well means that you can no longer use your afflictions, whatever they may be, to justify your behavior. Some people prefer unforgiveness to forgiveness, insecurity to security, anger to peace, fear to love. Sometimes we become institutionalized by our pain. We may not know who we are without it. Perhaps the walls are all too familiar. But for those who prefer freedom over prison bars, there is a way out.

So what's it going to be? Do you wish to get well? The answer to your breakthrough stands right before you. It's the outstretched arm of Jesus Christ who is ready to help you into the waters of His grace and love. He knows where you've been, what you've done, and what's been done to you. He understands. No one on the planet understands more than Him. After all, He became like us in every way (see Heb. 2:17). And even in spite of it all, He loves. He can't help but to love. It's His nature.

Remember, it is He who stood up in the synagogue to read from what was written of Himself in the words of the prophet Isaiah:

> *The Spirit of the Lord is upon Me, because He anointed Me to preach the gospel to the poor.* **He has sent Me to proclaim release to the captives,** *and recovery of sight to the blind,* **to set free those who are oppressed, to proclaim the favorable year of the Lord** (Luke 4:18-19).

The prison doors have flung open. It was for freedom that Christ set us free (see Gal. 5:1). This is the favorable year of the Lord, and His favor is poured out upon you through His great love demonstrated through His Son, Jesus Christ, who came to destroy the works of the enemy (see 1 John 3:8). Make no mistake, Jesus never once used sickness or the mistreatment of an individual to teach us some perverted lesson on how we should trust Him more. He healed all He came in contact with. Mistreatment, abuse, neglect—they are all instruments the enemy uses to destroy the possibility of believing in the love of God. But God wants to bring to an end the havoc that the enemy has been wreaking in your soul. He wants to crush all the lies of your past experiences and renew your mind with His love. I truly believe that He is waiting for us to invite Him into those locked away places in our heart. He wants to heal us, but He's patiently waiting for us to give Him the green light.

One of my favorite prayers throughout Scripture is the one that David prayed:

> *Search me, O God, and know my heart*; *try me and know my anxious thoughts; and see if there be any hurtful way in me*, *and lead me in the everlasting way* (Psalm 139:23-24).

David openly invited the Lord to see if there was anything hiding within his heart that was causing harm to not only himself but also to others. What's fascinating to me is that God knows our hearts (see 1 Sam. 16:7). Nothing is hidden from the Lord (see Heb. 4:13). Even though God knows all things, there's something about us inviting Him to openly search us. What we are largely saying is this: "I'm ready. I'm ready for You to come and show me what You already know. Let's get our hands dirty together."

Do you want to get well?

Are you ready to have the deepest and darkest places exposed?

Are you wanting to be led in the everlasting way of God's love and grace?

If so, I do believe it's as simple as praying David's prayer. I believe it's as simple as saying this:

> *Father, I'm in desperate need of Your healing touch. I confess that I've kept these things hidden, but I'm ready to expose them to Your love. I pray that You would come bring healing to the ways I've been treated in the past. Heal the memories. Heal the wounds.*
>
> *Not only that, I'm choosing to forgive the very people who have hurt me. I'm choosing to give them a gift they don't deserve in the same way I've received a gift that I don't deserve. I'm releasing them of the debt they owe me. I even choose to forgive myself of the things I've done that were motivated by the pain in my life.*
>
> *Jesus, come hold me.*
>
> *Holy Spirit, come fill me.*
>
> *Amen.*

ENDNOTES

1. For more information on Leona Lewis and her music, please visit her website: www.leonalewismusic.co.uk/us/.

2. A.W. Tozer, *Knowledge of the Holy* (New York, NY: HarperCollins, 1961), 1.

3. Raphael Erwin McManus, *Soul Cravings* (Nashville, TN: Thomas Nelson, 2008), Entry 14.

4. For more information on Bethany Dillon and her music, please visit her website: www.bethanydillon.com.

5. McManus, *Soul Cravings,* Entry 4.

Chapter 5

THE PRODIGAL BRIDE

I am no longer worthy to be called your son…
(Luke 15:19).

Two Brothers and a Father

The prodigal son story contained in Luke 15:11-32 has been used to illustrate Kingdom truths and realities in a variety of ways and in a variety of different contexts. It's probable to suspect, due to its popularity, that no passage of Scripture has been exhorted and taught on like this story about a father and his two sons. It is this very story that I'd like to use in this chapter to reveal what I believe to be a sad and unfortunate reality that is enveloping many of God's children today.

Let's recall the story together.

Jesus begins by explaining that a man had two sons. The younger of the two asks his father for his share of the estate that was to fall to him. After receiving his inheritance, the younger brother goes on a journey into a foreign land and wastes all of his money on what Jesus refers to as loose living.

Because of his newly acquired poverty and a recent famine that swept across the land he found himself to be living in, the younger brother decides to hire himself out to work for one of the citizens of that country to feed swine. The reality of his situation smacks him right between the eyes when he concludes that the very pigs he is feeding are living and eating better than he is. His only conclusion? Return home and confess his sins before his father and beg his dad to allow him to become one of his slaves.

While returning home, the younger brother rehearses his compelling argument:

> ...*Father, I have sinned against heaven, and in your sight;* **I am no longer worthy to be called your son**; *make me as one of your hired men* (Luke 15:18-19).

"I am no longer worthy."

What happened? The younger brother allowed his yesterday to determine his today and in that moment, his identity as his father's son was lost. His mistakes took the rightful place of his identity as his father's son. How many Christians are living this way today? How many sons and daughters of the Most High allow their failures and past sins to determine how they stand in relationship before their Father?

Because of his sin, the younger brother wanted to hide as a slave. "Make me as one of your hired men." Why is it that so many of us would prefer to be a slave rather than a friend of God? Why is it so hard to believe that the slate has been wiped clean? It was God Himself in Christ who was reconciling the world to Himself, not counting men's sins against them (see 2 Cor. 5:19). If He wasn't counting our sins against us, why do we hold them against ourselves? We must learn to allow the truth of what God has done to penetrate our hearts at the deepest level. His truth found in His Word far outweighs the reality of our circumstances and feelings.

"I am no longer worthy" is the standard by which many Christians live today. It's difficult to be a bride when you feel unworthy of the Bridegroom's affection.

And yet there was another brother in this story, wasn't there? An older brother—the brother, as we come to understand through the story, who never left his father's side. A faithful brother who did all that his father asked. This older brother became indignant when he heard of his younger brother's return and his father's response toward his younger son. He was appalled that his father celebrated rather than scorned and shooed his brother away. This kind of grace did not make sense to the older brother. Justice seemed to be his desire and the standard by which he lived.

Shortly after the younger brother returns and the father throws a party in his honor, the older brother becomes angry and refuses to join in the celebration. Disturbed by his older son's absence, the father seeks to find his son.

The father finds his son, arms crossed and brow wrinkled, outside where the party was taking place. After pleading with his son to join the festivities, the older brother replies this way:

> ...*Look! For so many years **I have been serving you and I have never neglected a command of yours**; and yet you have never given me a young goat, so that I might celebrate with my friends; but when this son of yours came, who has devoured your wealth with prostitutes, you killed the fattened calf for him* (Luke 15:29-30).

"I have been serving you and I have never neglected a command of yours."

Just like the younger brother, the older brother utilizes the past tense in his argument to prove that his yesterday determines his today as well. Where the younger brother felt unworthy because of his actions, the older brother feels a sense of entitlement because of his keeping of every one of his father's commands. Truly, the older brother believes he's owed something and he's looking to collect. Just like the younger brother wanted to hide by becoming a slave, the older brother hid behind his works.

How many Christians today are hiding behind their works? How many Christians feel entitled to something because of their faithfulness in attending church and serving and never neglecting a command of God? How many Christians judge a fellow brother or sister on the basis of their behavior as if their standard of living is the measuring stick?

What I find to be so fascinating about this story in Luke 15 is the father's response, which is who this story is largely about. Many of us are familiar with the father's response toward the younger brother, which is why so many of us are familiar with the title of this parable: "The Prodigal Son." We know that the father blows off his younger son's big speech about not being worthy and envelops him in hugs and kisses, clothes him with the best robe, places a ring on his finger, and shod his feet with sandals (see Luke 15:22). It's one of the greatest images of grace and love found in the Scriptures. It offers hope to any one of us who has strayed in our relationship with our Father. It draws a picture that reveals that there is no end to God's grace. His arms are always opened wide.

I've always identified with the younger brother because my life of running and hiding mirrors his. But I also find myself taken aback by the father's response to the older brother. This is what he tells his oldest son: *"Son, you have always been with me, and **all that is mine is yours"** (Luke 15:31).*

The older son didn't have because he didn't ask. He didn't have to earn a thing. It was always his. He could have asked for his share of the estate in the same way his younger brother did. But just like his younger brother, neither of them *knew* the love of their father. If they did, they would have dismissed their argument. It's in this lack of understanding of our heavenly Father's love that we find ourselves left with these two conclusions:

1. I am no longer worthy of love.

2. I have to earn love.

Make no mistake; it was the father's love that was the common theme in this parable. Sadly, so many Christians are cowering in shame or posing behind their performance. This leads to a mixed-up identity that creates feelings of insecurity and inferiority.

Insecurity says, "I don't know who I am." Inferiority says, "I don't know my value."

The truth is that both my identity and my value are found in the love of my Father. When I *know* Him, I know who I am. Not only that, but when I know how great His love is for me, I am willing to make myself known to Him. I will not hide behind my shame or my performance. Because neither brother knew the love of their father, they lost sight of both their identity and value. The younger brother went from son to slave in his thinking. The older brother reveals his lack of understanding by never asking his father for what was rightfully his to begin with.

As sons and daughters of God through faith in Christ, we've been given an inheritance (see Eph. 1:11). Paul prays that we would know the riches of the glory of His inheritance in the saints (see Eph. 1:18). First Peter 1:4 tells us that part of the inheritance is eternal life. Ephesians 1:13-14 says that the Holy Spirit was given as a pledge of our inheritance. Because we are sons and daughters, we are co-heirs with Christ (see Rom. 8:17). This tells me that all that is Christ's is mine. I have access to the same things Jesus did. There's an open heaven above me. But how many of us are accessing the riches of God's Kingdom now and how many of us are waiting to die to receive our inheritance?

A few weeks ago, I was talking with my dad about adopting. My wife and I had gotten pregnant with our first daughter after trying with great difficulty. To be honest, the odds were so stacked against us medically that it's a miracle that our daughter, Emma, is here today. Since that time, Nicole and I have talked about adopting. Our belief is that it's better to save a life that no one wants than it is to exhaust resources on something that only God can do anyway (see Mark 5:25-29). Orphans are, after all, very near and dear to the heart of God. It's He who is a Father to the fatherless and makes a home for the lonely (see Ps. 68:5-6).

After discussing the idea of adoption with my father, he came at me with this crazy comment: "Son, if you and Nicole adopt, I will give you $10,000."

The reason why my dad is willing to give such a generous gift is because his and God's philosophies are the same. What's the point of waiting to give an inheritance when you can give it right now to help usher in the Kingdom of God? My dad didn't come up with this on his own. This is a Kingdom principle. He learned it through his relationship with God.

In the same way that my dad is willing to give $10,000, God wants to give you far above and beyond all that you could ask or think (see Eph. 3:20).

Our Identity and Value

When Jesus said, "I am the truth," He was saying that He is the truth about who the Father is and who we are (see John 14:6). He was declaring that He is the truth about our value. Dan Mohler of Neck Ministries can often be heard making this statement: "You are worth the blood of Jesus." If this is true, it changes everything.

Dan will often use this analogy to make his point. Who of you would spend $100,000 for a $20,000 car? That would be silly. Yet Jesus shed His blood for you. You must be a big deal to God. You only pay a great price for something that's of great value.

These statements are true and they change everything.

The cost of the ring that Jesus places on my finger is the price of what it cost Him at Calvary—His very life.

This is a God who loves me.

This is a God who wants me to know Him.

Are you beginning to hear the cry of His heart for you? Are you beginning to understand that this thing is bigger than simply praying a prayer to get to Heaven?

It's a relationship with the God who created the universe, and He's calling out for you.

PART II

Can You Hear the Sound?

Chapter 6

THE GLORY OF HIS PRESENCE

*He who has My commandments and keeps them is the one who loves Me; and he who loves Me will be loved by My Father, and **I will love him and will disclose Myself to him*** (John 14:21).

Not Again!

How I met my wife, Nicole, is actually a funny story. Believe it or not, I dated her best friend, Holly, prior to our own courtship. If that wasn't weird enough, my wife went on a date once with *my* best friend. All of this took place while we were in college together at our beloved Alma Mater, Millersville University.

Holly and I broke up in December of 2000. Our relationship only lasted for three months, but it was a painful separation. I truly believed that Holly was the woman God had wanted me to marry.

When you're convinced that the person you are dating is "the one" and the relationship comes to a quick halt, you're left feeling not only devastated, but completely confused. How could this happen if this was the person God wanted me to be with? I guess the simple answer is that Holly wasn't meant to be the one who I would be saying "I do" with at the altar.

Because most of my interaction with Nicole occurred while Holly and I were dating, I didn't see Nicole at all for the greater part of eight months while at Millersville after Holly and I broke up. Then, during the first day of classes in the fall semester of 2001, the strangest thing happened. I ran into Nicole.

Please keep in mind that I am a senior in college during this part of the story. Technically speaking, I should know my way around campus like the back of my hand. But for some strange reason on this day that I would "by coincidence" run into Nicole, I was totally lost. I can still recall what happened that day as if it happened yesterday.

I was walking around in Byerly Hall desperately seeking to find my class. Judging by the time on my watch, I was running late. I hate running late. This only served to quicken my fanaticism to find my class and fast. I was looking for classroom 321 (or something like that). The weird thing is that I knew Byerly Hall to only have two floors. How could there be classrooms in the 300s? There was no third floor!

To my own embarrassment and defeat, I succumbed to asking a professor in the hallway where classroom 321 was located. She glanced down at the paper I was holding that contained my scheduling information and simply stated that I was looking at the course number (which is used to identify that particular class's level of difficulty), not the classroom number. She pointed out that the room I was looking for was 105.

After making my way into my class, I noticed that nearly every seat was taken. I quickly sat down in the front, completely relieved to even be in the class. Shortly after I sat down, I heard a faint whisper calling my name, coming from the back of the class. I turned to see who it was. Wouldn't you know it, there sat Nicole with a huge smile, waving her hand at me in excitement. I smiled in return and waved back.

At the end of our exchange, the professor began to take roll call. I half listened as he read off name after name, only coming back into consciousness when my name was mentioned. Once finished, the professor went on to share some basic information about the class and briefly went through the syllabus.

To my surprise, he released us within 15 minutes of the class's start time. I hopped up out of my chair, eager to talk to Nicole. But when I began to make my way to the back of the class, I noticed that she was gone! Why would she leave so soon and not stick around to catch up? This bothered me. It didn't make sense. One minute she's smiling and waving frantically at me and the next it's as if she was never in the class to begin with.

Needless to say, I was on a mission to find out what happened to Nicole. I returned home, hopped on the computer, and e-mailed her. That same day, Nicole replied and said that while the professor was going through the roll, she realized that her name wasn't mentioned. Nervously, she examined her schedule to find out that she was in the wrong class! What are the chances? (Are you starting to see the irony of this story? I was late to the class that she wasn't supposed to be in!)

After a few more correspondences over e-mail, Nicole and I began to hang out together, which led to the blossoming of a beautiful friendship. She and I did many things together. We practically spent the entire fall semester either at her apartment with her roommates or vice versa. All the while, I was developing some pretty intense feelings for her. These "feelings" were exceeding that of the friendship level, and at the same time a dilemma was rising up inside of me. Some of you know exactly what it is that I'm going to say next.

The dilemma was this: Do I tell Nicole how I really feel? What if she doesn't feel the same way? But what if she does? Surely if we were to begin dating and it didn't work out we would maintain our friendship because it has such a firm foundation.

How many of you had a conversation like that with yourself over someone you were close to?

Here's the thing, however—I had already been down this road before.

I walked this path back in the eleventh grade with a girl I was convinced would go for the idea of "taking our friendship to the next level." Unfortunately, it blew up in my face. Not only did she not go for the idea, our friendship crumbled shortly thereafter.

Was I willing to risk the same possibility with Nicole?

On February 14, 2002 (on Valentine's Day of all days!), I asked Nicole the same question I had asked that girl back in high school: "Would you like to be more than friends?"

There was a long pause. Minutes felt like an eternity. *Oh no, I thought. Not again!* After that interlude of awkward silence, Nicole gave her answer: "I'll have to think about it."

Ugh!

Honestly, I believed her response was a gentler way of saying "no."

It's over, I thought to myself. *There's no way she's going to say yes.* But because she and I are married, we know how the story ends, don't we? Two weeks after I popped the question, she said yes! And now, six years later, we are happily married with a beautiful two-year-old daughter, Emma.

More Than Just Friends

In John 15:15, Jesus says this:

> *No longer do I call you slaves, for the slave does not know what his master is doing;* **but I have called you friends,** *for all things that I have heard from My Father I have made known to you* (John 15:15).

Jesus calls us friends. This is simply stunning. How great it is to have the One who created it all and for whom it was all created call us friends (see Col. 1:16). It is in this friendship that God reveals things to us like John 15:15 suggests. Friends share things together, including their very lives.

But I believe, just like with my desire for Nicole, that God wants to be more than just friends. I believe He desires intimacy with us in such a way that results in the enjoyment of each other's company as well as disclosure of the self.

Recently, God revealed to me a deeper revelation of the following passage of Scripture that helps to illustrate this point:

> ...If anyone wishes to come after Me, he must deny himself, and take up his cross and follow Me (Mark 8:34).

The truth is that I was never created for me. I was created for Him. I was created to be loved by Him and to enjoy Him. When I decide to come after Him (pursue Him), deny myself, and take up my cross, I'm declaring that I am dying to myself. When I die to myself, I am no longer married *to* myself. Before Christ, I was the only one I was living for. I was married to me. In Christ, I've died. I've divorced myself and now I'm ready to be joined with Him. I'm ready to become "one flesh" with Him. I love how the apostle Paul says it in Galatians:

> I have been crucified with Christ; and it is no longer I who live, but Christ lives in me; and the life which I now live in the flesh I live by faith in the Son of God, who loved me and gave Himself up for me (Galatians 2:20).

This is how intimate He wants to be. This is how intimate I want to be. Throughout history, our awareness of His feelings toward us has quickened through the manifestation of His presence in five concrete ways. Please note, there have been many times in Scripture where God has appeared to or spoken to individuals, but I will be focusing on what I believe to be the five ways after the Fall of man where God has manifested Himself to a company of people where deep revelations of His character were released through each manifestation.

It's through these manifestations that God was continually inviting us to know Him and experience Him in a fresh, new way. Like I said at the beginning of this book, the invitation to know Him at a deeper level did not end with our praying of the sinner's prayer. Relationships do not end after the introduction. That would be silly. If you were to get anything out of this book, please get this: God is inviting you deeper and deeper into Himself. Accept the invitation.

Let's take a look at the five concrete examples after the Fall of man where God has manifested Himself in such a way to reveal greater revelation about who He is and how He feels about us.

Living Between the Trees

A few years ago, I had watched a NOOMA video called "Trees." In this video, Rob Bell, senior pastor of Mars Hill Bible Church and creator of the NOOMA video series, explains that since the Fall of man, we are currently living between the trees.[1] Although he speaks of trees in the pluralistic sense, it is merely one tree in two separate locations—the tree of life. The following diagram should help:

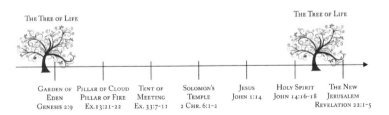

THE TREE OF LIFE · THE TREE OF LIFE

GARDEN OF EDEN GENESIS 2:9 · PILLAR OF CLOUD PILLAR OF FIRE EX. 13:21-22 · TENT OF MEETING EX. 33:7-11 · SOLOMON'S TEMPLE 2 CHR. 6:1-2 · JESUS JOHN 1:14 · HOLY SPIRIT JOHN 14:16-18 · THE NEW JERUSALEM REVELATION 22:1-5

This diagram represents the process by which God began to work His way back into our lives since the Fall of man in the garden. Where we were once positioned to eat of the tree of life in the garden of Eden, we will once again be co-inhabitors with that very tree once again in the New Jerusalem. I do not believe, however, that all things will once again be like they were in the garden. Revelation 21:1-5 discusses a new Heaven and a new earth and the idea that God is making all things new. The new Jerusalem will be a new reality, unlike that of the garden.

Each manifestation of His presence resulted in a new revelation of who God is and how He feels about us. I will not go into an abundance of detail regarding each manifestation, but I will help you understand the revelation that was released through each time God revealed Himself.

Pillars of Cloud and Fire

When God had delivered the Israelites from 400 years of Egyptian oppression, He appeared before them as a pillar of cloud by day and a pillar of fire by night to give them light, that they might travel by day and night (see Exod. 13:21). The revelation that was released through this manifestation was this: *God is a deliverer*. Not only does He deliver, He guides. He protects. He leads.

The Tent of Meeting

While Israel was wandering for 40 years in the wilderness, God commanded them to construct what was known as the tent of meeting. The tent of meeting was literally the portable dwelling place of God. As the Israelites moved around, they were able to deconstruct and reconstruct the tent.

It was in the tent of meeting where Aaron and his sons would minister. It was in the tent of meeting where the ark of the testimony dwelt. And it was in the tent of meeting where God met with Moses face to face.

Because the tent of meeting was mobile and was with them in the wilderness, the revelation that was found within God's dwelling in the tent of meeting was this: *God encamps around His people.* On at least one occasion, Moses was unable to enter the tent of meeting because the glory of the Lord filled the tabernacle (see Exod. 40:34-38). In other words, there were times when the presence of God surrounded Israel in greater measure.

Solomon's Temple

Whereas the tent of meeting was the portable resting place of God, Solomon's temple represented a fixed dwelling—the perpetual, established presence of God. Although it had always been King David's dream to build the temple, God told him not to because he was a man of bloodshed (see 1 Chron. 28:3). Rather, the commission to build a more permanent place to house the presence of God fell to David's son, Solomon. Without going into all the details of the temple, let me point out that the revelation that was released through the building of this incredible fixture was this: *God dwells among us.*

God wants to be with His people. He's always wanted to be with His people, and as their understanding of this grew, His presence became more fixed and more tangible.

Jesus

*And the **Word became flesh**, and dwelt among us, and **we saw His glory**, glory as of the only begotten from the Father, **full of grace and truth*** (John 1:14).

God in the flesh. What could be more beautiful than the image of God stepping down to reveal to sinful humanity their worth and His affection toward them? Truly, this is the unthinkable. The One who created it all becoming like that which He created, subjected to temptation and the same ailments that befall every human being—hunger, thirst, exhaustion, etc. Philippians says it this way:

> *...Although He existed in the form of God, did not regard equality with God a thing to be grasped, but **emptied Himself**, taking the form of a bond-servant, and being made in the likeness of men. Being found in appearance as a man, He humbled Himself by becoming obedient to the point of death, even death on a cross* (Philippians 2:6-8).

Why do it? There can be only one logical explanation—love.

*For **God so loved the world**, that He gave His only begotten Son...* (John 3:16).

The revelation of God that manifested through Jesus Christ was this: *God loves us.* He loved so much that He gave. The fullness of God in Christ was at all times drawing men to Himself (see Matt. 15:29-31). It was through His great love that people were continually being healed, delivered, and forgiven.

As I stated earlier in a previous chapter, Jesus is the exact representation of the Father (see Heb. 1:3). Not only that, but Jesus also only ever did what He saw His Father doing (see John 5:19). So the only conclusion can be this: Whatever we see Jesus doing is exactly what His Father was doing. However He responded is how the Father responded. John says it best when he writes this in his Gospel:

> *No one has seen God at any time; the only begotten God who is in the bosom of the Father,* ***He has explained Him*** (John 1:18).

Through Jesus we come to know the Father. Through Jesus we come to know ourselves.

The Holy Spirit

The greatest commentary on the Holy Spirit (who He is and what He does) is contained in Jesus' words found in John 14 and 16. It is at this juncture that we find the manifest presence of God the greatest it has ever been, and it is in this revelation that we find ourselves currently living. Because the Holy Spirit dwells within each and every believer (see John 14:16-18,23; Eph. 1:13), the Word refers to us as being the "Body of Christ"—the literal, manifest presence of God on the planet (see I Cor. 12:27).

Up to this point in time, we've witnessed the transition of God's presence from the temporary to the permanent. Whereas God once dwelt inside the Holy of Holies found within Solomon's temple, He now lives in us in the person of the Holy Spirit. First Corinthians 6:19 goes so far as to make this stunning comment— we are now the temple of the Holy Spirit. We house the actual presence of God.

John writes in his Gospel this amazing statement:

> *Jesus answered and said to him, "If anyone loves Me, he will keep My word; and My Father will love him, and **We will come to him and make Our abode with him**"* (John 14:23).

I pray that you are able to grasp with me the revelation that the Father and Son through the Holy Spirit have chosen to abide within us. Jesus says this about this very reality:

> *But I tell you the truth, **it is to your advantage that I go away**; for if I do not go away, the Helper will not come to you; but if I go, I will send Him to you* (John 16:7).

Let's be honest. This statement that *"it is to your advantage that I go away"* doesn't make a whole lot of sense. Wouldn't we rather have Jesus? Wouldn't we rather have God in the flesh—a God we could talk to face to face, touch, and curl up next to like John did? The truth is this—*it is to our advantage* that we have the Holy Spirit.

Lest we forget, it's the Holy Spirit who does the following:

- He teaches us all things and brings to remembrance all that Jesus said (see John 14:26).

- He testifies about Jesus (see John 15:26).

- He convicts the world concerning sin and righteousness and judgment (see John 16:8).

- He guides us into all truth (see John 16:13).

- He empowers us to be God's supernatural witnesses throughout all the earth (see Acts 1:8).

- He births the Kingdom of God within us through peace, joy, and righteousness (see Rom. 14:17).

All of these things the Holy Spirit does for us. It *truly is* to our advantage that the Father has sent the Helper. There is no greater reality than God in us, which leads me to point out the fifth and final revelation of God contained in the manifest presence of the Holy Spirit living in us. *All that we have witnessed the presence of God doing throughout human history lives inside of you and me. Everything is available to us.*

The very glory that prevented people like Moses and Solomon from entering the tent of meeting and the temple lives in me. The ability of God to deliver me and lead me like the pillar of cloud and pillar of fire lives in me. Let's take it a step further—the very Spirit that raised Christ from the dead and enabled Him to heal the sick, raise the dead, and cast out demons *lives inside of me* (see Rom. 8:11). That's amazing. What could possibly limit us? Only a lack of revelation surrounding these truths.

God Encounters

Each one of these five manifestations resulted in God encounters that forever changed the way the audiences perceived God and themselves. This is the nature of the encounter. We can expect to be different. We can expect to be transformed. Encounters lead to renewed minds which lead to outward transformation (see Rom. 12:2).

Each time Jesus performed a miracle by healing the sick, casting out demons, raising the dead, or feeding the multitudes, those who were present were radically impacted by the love of God for them that was manifested through the Son of God. When Jesus delivered me from years of drug addiction, I was never the same. Everything changed. God was more real in that moment than ever before. *It was the encounter.* God met me right where I was in the midst of my suffering and pain and said in that very moment, "I love you, son." From that point on, I decided to live my life for that kind of God—a God who can take all things and work them together for good (see Rom. 8:28). A God who has taken my history and brought deliverance and healing through the power of His testimony in my life.

What God has done for one person, He can do for another. *"...For the testimony of Jesus is the spirit of prophecy"* (Rev. 19:10).

All Who Are Thirsty

On Thursday, December 3, 2009, I encountered God in a way I never had before and still haven't to this very day. I was attending the School of Impartation and Healing[2] that centered on deliverance and disbelief at the Global School of Supernatural Ministry. I had been invited to attend this conference by a good friend of mine, Jason Hostetter, pastor of Windward Ministries in New Berlin, Pennsylvania. I'll be forever indebted to Jason for inviting me.

During the Thursday evening session of the conference, Randy Clark, founder of Global Awakening, shared a message that he has preached many times before called "How Thirsty Are You?" This was, however, the first time I have ever heard Randy share this message.

During this talk, Randy shared intimate details about his history with God—the hurts, the joys, how God has used him, and where he finds himself today. It was wonderful!

His message ended with a time of impartation—the act of the laying on hands for the baptism of the Holy Spirit and/or the activation of the gifts of the Spirit within the believer. For more information on the subject of impartation, please refer to Randy Clark's book, *There Is More: Reclaiming the Power of Impartation.*[3]

The sole purpose of Randy's message was to stir a hunger and a thirst within us to have more of God in our lives. He concluded his talk by stating that he was going to pray and invite the Holy Spirit to come. He shared that those of us who were truly thirsty would begin to experience physical manifestations of God's presence. He said that some of us may feel or experience the following:

- Heat in our hands
- Crying
- Laughter
- Electricity coursing through our bodies
- A heaviness that could feel as if we were being pushed down
- Shaking or trembling
- Tingling in our hands (similar to the sensation when a member of your body falls asleep)

Although this list is not exhaustive, they just so happen to be the most common ways that Randy has seen the Holy Spirit touch people in response to their desire for more.

Sure enough, before Randy even prayed for the Holy Spirit to come, my hands were both tingling and sweating. A heaviness came upon me that resulted in a feeling as if someone were pushing down upon my shoulders. Something was happening!

After Randy finished praying, he invited those of us who were experiencing the various things he listed prior to praying to come forward. He shared that the Holy Spirit was wanting to do something special within us. Whereas I didn't understand at first why the Holy Spirit was touching only a select few of us, I believe that I do understand what was happening then much better today. It is my opinion that the Holy Spirit was moving upon those of us who truly counted the cost, those who were wanting more of God and wanting to be used by Him. These were the hungry and thirsty who were about to be satisfied (see Matt. 5:6).

With tingling and sweat in my hands and a heaviness upon my shoulders, I came forward. Randy explained that he and the leaders of the conference were going to lay hands on us and pray for the filling of the Holy Spirit. Before I go any further in this story, let me make this distinction for those who might be confused.

In John 20:22, Jesus breathed on the disciples and said to them, *"Receive the Holy Spirit."* In Acts 2, which we commonly refer to as "Pentecost," those who were assembled in the house were *filled* with the Holy Spirit (see Acts 2:4). Throughout the Book of Acts, we see believers being filled with the Holy Spirit through the laying on of the apostles' hands.

I believe that every believer has *received* the Holy Spirit (see John 14:16-18,23; Eph. 1:13), but I also believe that there is a difference between receiving and being filled. I believe that it is this "filling" that is referred to as the baptism of the Holy Spirit and is required to become God's supernatural witnesses throughout all the ends of the earth (see Acts 1:8).

OK. Back to the story.

There I stood, hands out in front of me in a posture ready to receive whatever it was that God wanted to do with me. Coming down off of the platform toward me was Will Hart, founder of Hart Ministries, one of the instructors for the conference.[4] I was happy to see Will approach me because I really enjoyed his teachings. I connected with his zeal and outgoing, exuberant personality.

What happened next was so dramatic and unlike anything that I had ever experienced before that it's difficult to explain. Will placed both of his hands on my face, spoke one word, "Fill," and blew in my face. Immediately, I dropped to one knee, my hands curled up against my chest, and I fell face forward onto the floor. My breathing immediately quickened to the rhythm and intensity of a woman in labor. I shook and shook and shook under the power of God. I cried under the power of God. It was beautiful. The God of the universe was touching me!

I'm not sure how long the experience lasted; I can only tell you the fruit of it. The first thing that I noticed was newness of life in my relationship with God. It was as if someone hooked jumper cables up to my spirit and released a charge so great that my very being was filled with the power of God. Three times in my life I felt like I had been born again. Please don't take what I'm about to say as being blasphemous. I understand that we are only "born again" *one time* through our receiving of the Lord Jesus Christ. However, I can think of no other phrase or wording to best capture those moments when I encountered God in a way I never had before. The first time was through the deliverance of my drug use and what I believe to be the first time I received Jesus Christ into my life. The second time I felt born again was through my counseling process. It was during the process of my inner healing where things came alive for what seemed like the first time. The trees looked different. There was a bounce in my step. It felt like nothing could touch me. The third time was this experience from the conference that I am recalling.

Other fruit from this experience was found in my deliverance from a 20-year bout with pornography and a greater desire for ministry. I fell more and more in love with God. My relationship with Him immediately soared into greater realms of intimacy. Not only that, I began to see God's power manifest through me as I prayed for people to be healed and to be filled with the Holy Spirit. Not only did I *encounter* the glory of His presence, I was now experiencing His glory flowing through me to others through the power of the Holy Spirit. I still experience it today. Make no mistake, this wasn't what so many in the church want to downplay as being some kind of "high." This wasn't some mountaintop experience and I'm waiting to come back down off the mountain. This is everyday life.

These kinds of experiences are reserved for every believer. This is how much God loves you. He literally wants to rock your world. He wants to fill you with His Holy Spirit and wants you to continually be filled (see Eph. 5:18). He wants to manifest Himself to you in this way—the greatest way we've seen to date throughout history.

This whole concept of God living in us in the person of the Holy Spirit has actually resulted in something that the world has never seen before. Read Paul's words in Second Corinthians:

> *Therefore if anyone is in Christ, **he is a new creature**; the old things passed away; behold, new things have come* (2 Corinthians 5:17).

You are a new creature. There has never been anything like you on the planet. This is simply stunning. Paul goes on to say this: *"For neither is circumcision anything, nor uncircumcision, **but a new creation"** (Gal. 6:15).

The only thing that matters is that through Christ, I've become a new creation. The old is gone and the new has come. I am *literally* filled with the Holy Spirit and all that I have seen the presence of God doing throughout human history lives inside of me.

Get This!

It is my personal belief that when we are able to grasp the reality of these truths, we will not only be awakened to the power that lives within us, but we will also be compelled, controlled by the love that lives within us and is constantly being poured out upon us (see 2 Cor. 5:14).

This is how much God loves you: He's chosen to make His home in you. He's chosen to reveal Himself to you. He's chosen to empower you and He's chosen to be more than just friends. But do we? Do we want to be more than just friends?

Let's talk about this even further in the next two chapters, but first let's read some testimonies of those who truly wanted to be more than just friends with God.

ENDNOTES

1. For more information on Rob Bell and the NOOMA video series, please visit his websites: www.robbell.com and www.marshill.org.

2. For more information on these schools and other upcoming Global Awakening events, please visit Global Awakening's website: www.globalawakening.com.

3. Randy Clark, *There Is More: Reclaiming the Power of Impartation* (Mechanicsburg, PA: Global Awakening, 2006).

4. For more information on Will Hart and his ministry, please visit his website: www.hartministries.org.

Chapter 7

NOTHING SAYS "I LOVE YOU" LIKE VALENTINE'S DAY

*It happened that while Apollos was at Corinth, Paul passed through the upper country and came to Ephesus, and found some disciples. He said to them, "**Did you receive the Holy Spirit when you believed...**" (Acts 19:1-2)*

Do You Think It Will Work for Me?

A few weeks after my encounter with the Holy Spirit at the School of Impartation and Healing, I went to visit my best friend, Adam (the same Adam from the beginning of the book) in York, Pennsylvania. What was originally intended to be just a "time of hanging out and playing video games" suddenly turned into something I had never seen before.

Adam was in a very difficult place. The church he was serving at (Praise Community Church) as the senior high youth pastor had just gone through a horrific season of transition. Because of the web of lies and deceit that was exposed, the senior pastor was asked to step down. By default, the role of senior pastor fell into Adam's lap—a responsibility that he was happy to receive. It wasn't so much the new position that was difficult for Adam; rather, it was the hurt and disappointment of learning that his pastor, a close friend of his, was engaged in some unthinkable things behind the scenes.

Emotionally, Adam was drained. Spiritually, Adam was confused.

While partaking in one of our favorite pastimes (playing video games), I shared with Adam what had happened to me at the conference. To be honest, I had no idea how he was going to receive what I was saying. I was actually afraid that he wouldn't believe me, or worse yet, think I was crazy. Up to this point, everything that I had described in the previous chapter had not been my or Adam's experience. But because of our relationship, Adam took to heart all that I had to say.

Shortly after I spilled the beans about my encounter, we turned the video games off and made our way upstairs. Our conversation continued at the kitchen table. We jumped back and forth between my experience at the conference and the plight that Adam and the people of Praise Community Church found themselves in. Finally,

Adam popped the question I had been nervously anticipating: "Do you think it will work for me?"

Before I knew what happened, my right hand was resting on Adam's back and I was praying, "Come, Holy Spirit."

All I could think was this: *What if it doesn't happen?* Oddly enough, I would later learn that Adam was thinking the same thing.

At first, nothing was happening, but I kept praying. There's something about desperation that draws the very presence of God. It wasn't long before Adam was bending forward at the waist. It was at this point that Adam would later explain that he gave himself over fully to what the Holy Spirit wanted to do. He said it felt as if the gravitational pull that was causing him to bend forward was the size of Jupiter. As a result, Adam found himself glued to the floor. He couldn't move for at least 15 minutes.

Surprisingly, Adam's visitation didn't end when he was able to get up. His experience with the Holy Spirit lasted the greater part of the day! I watched him cry. I watched him laugh. It was as if I were watching the pendulum of a clock swing from side to side. The Holy Spirit was doing a major work within Adam! It was one of the greatest God encounters I had ever seen. He was truly drunk with the Holy Spirit!

It is my opinion that Adam was equipped more that day for ministry than in all of his years of seminary training. Don't get me wrong, I'm not criticizing seminary education. I myself am seminary trained and wouldn't trade that for the world. In fact, I believe that Adam was experiencing a great merger of the Word (his training at seminary) and the Spirit. The fruit of Adam's experience was an immediate launch into supernatural ministry as well as the healing from previous family wounds.

Beyond Belief

Not too long after Adam's encounter with the Holy Spirit, I began to receive many requests to return to York and pray for people through the laying on of hands. The hunger for more of God and to encounter Him was breeding among the people of Praise Community Church. Even though I explained to Adam that it was within him to lay hands on people and pray for the baptism of the Holy Spirit, he felt much more comfortable charging me with this task. I quickly became known as "the guy" through whom all of this was happening among the people at Praise.

As more and more people were hearing of not only Adam's encounter but others as well, Adam began a teaching series at Praise called "Beyond Belief" in January of 2010. Slowly, throughout these teachings, Adam began to expose the rest of the congregation to the supernatural and to what he and some other members of Praise had already experienced. The goals of the series were simple:

1. Challenge peoples' preconceived beliefs, and

2. Raise the expectations of the congregants by sharing personal testimonies.

A Taste of Things to Come

The efforts of Adam's sowing reached their time of harvest on Sunday, February 14, 2010—Valentine's Day! Adam had done such a great job of stirring up spiritual hunger within his congregation that he requested me to come and speak to the people of Praise Community Church during both Sunday morning services and a special Sunday evening service where I was to lead a time of impartation.

During the morning service, I had taught on why we (Christians) can and must walk supernaturally. Most of the information I presented came from what I had acquired at the School of Impartation and Healing conference and through Bill Johnson's book, *When Heaven Invades Earth.*[1] The congregation loved it. "Amen" and "that's right" could be heard coming from those in the seats. The people of Praise Community were so hungry that some didn't want to wait until later that evening to receive prayer.

One man, Dave Lauer, was so hungry for more of God that he walked right up to me between services and asked, "Would you pray for me?"

"Sure," I said. "What would you like me to pray for?"

Dave replied, "More."

I placed my right hand on Dave's left shoulder and I got no more than a few words out of my mouth when this approximately 6 foot, 4 inch, 240-pound monster of a man came falling forward into me. I braced myself, caught him the best I could, and lowered him to the ground. When I looked up, I noticed that a line was forming.

Some of the people wanted prayer for healing. Others were following in Dave's footsteps with wanting more. It was a glorious time, but it was only the tip of the iceberg of what God was preparing to do that evening.

Corporate Impartation

Adam and I returned to the church at 6 p.m. after an afternoon of relaxing and sharing testimonies. The people of Praise were going to return at 7 p.m. for the impartation service, so Adam and I arrived an hour early, armed with coffee, to pray and get ready for the evening. It wasn't long, however, before people began to file into the auditorium.

Anticipation saturated the air. These were the people who wanted more of God. These were the people who wanted to be more than just friends.

Worship began promptly at 7 p.m. Adam and I made our way to one of the back corners of the auditorium to observe what God was up to. One of the first things that Adam and I had noticed was a visual change in the atmosphere. It appeared as if the air in that room physically manifested itself. The air was dense and a misty fog lingered above the heads of those assembled. "This is incredible," I said to myself.

God was in that place.

After worship, I made my way onto the stage and shared a message titled "Pressing In," a title I had borrowed from Randy Clark, but not the same material. It was a message that centered on the apostle Peter. When it came to understanding the Kingdom of God, Peter either hit a home run or struck out. Sometimes his zeal got ahead of his revelation (such as when he only walked on the water for a short period of time). But he was a man who truly wanted to know the Lord and to be used by Him. God is drawn to people like Peter, no matter how many mistakes they make. Second Chronicles says it this way:

*For the eyes of the Lord move to and fro throughout the earth that He may strongly support **those whose heart is completely His**...* (2 Chronicles 16:9).

The Lord is not only looking for people who want to be used by Him; He's also looking for laid-down lovers—those who are willing to die to themselves in order to know Him at a greater level. This point is illustrated in no greater way than in the conversation between Jesus and Peter in the last chapter of John's Gospel.

After Peter had denied his Lord three times, he went away feeling ashamed and unworthy. In fact, the Bible says that he returned to the one thing we find him doing prior to his meeting Jesus—fishing (see John 21:3). Men only return to their former life when they feel inadequate or incapable in their new life. It is my opinion that Peter felt like he blew it, he failed, and the only logical thing to do was to return to what he had always known—fishing.

While Peter was fishing with Thomas and Nathanael, Jesus appeared on the beach. The Lord instructed them where to drop their nets, and when they did as Jesus said they discovered that they were unable to haul in the great number of fish (see John 21:4-6). It is here where we find Peter doing what he does best. He concludes that the man standing on the beach is Jesus. As a result, he is the first one out of the boat. Before Thomas and Nathanael could act, Peter had swum half way to the beach.

Soon after a breakfast consisting of bread and fish, Peter and Jesus engage in that all-too-familiar conversation consisting of those three infamous questions: *"Simon, son of John, do you love Me?"* Each time, Peter responds the same way: *"Yes, Lord; You know that I love You"* (John 21:15). After Jesus tells Peter three times to tend/shepherd His sheep, Jesus indicates the kind of death that Peter will die (see John 21:18). In other words, Jesus was trying to show Peter that the love he would have for his Friend would cause him to lay his life down for Him. In this, Jesus said, there is no greater love (see John 15:13).

The cost of following Jesus is denying yourself. It's death. It's dying to the very thing that was hand packaged to us through the fall of man: the self life (self-righteousness, self-centeredness, self-pity, etc.). In Peter's case, this was quite literal. Although most of us will not have to die a martyr's death, I wanted to make it clear to the people of Praise Community Church that there is a cost to wanting more of God. When you pour water into an already full glass of orange juice, the water begins to push out the orange juice and take its place in the glass. When you want more of God, His presence comes and pushes out the things that are filling our lives and He takes their place.

After the message was finished, I instructed the 120-plus people on what was going to happen next. I explained that I was going to do the very same thing I had witnessed Randy Clark do back on that life-changing Thursday evening, December 3, 2009. I told the people that the Holy Spirit was going to come and that some of them would feel or experience His presence in multiple ways. I also shared that those for whom this would be true are those who have truly counted the cost and desperately wanted more of God no matter what.

I asked those whom I had prayed for in the past from Praise Community to join me on the stage. I wanted them to see how you could actually see what the Father was doing by watching these visible manifestations and to help me during this time of ministry. The moment I started to pray, you could both hear and see what

God was doing. Some people were crying loudly. Some were shaking. Others were bending forward under the weight of His glory. The sight was amazing. But there was one manifestation that stood out among all the rest. It was one that shook Adam to the core. A young woman, both crying and shaking, began wailing in a way I never heard before. It was the cry of hunger pangs. And it was this manifestation that immediately changed the atmosphere of the auditorium. The air was pregnant with God's presence.

I then called forward those whom the Holy Spirit was touching. One after the other, these people encountered God in a very radical way. After we finished praying for the first group of people, we called forward anyone else who wanted to be filled with the Holy Spirit. We prayed for hours. Man, woman, and child alike were encountering God everywhere. These were the people the Lord was looking for. These were the laid-down lovers who wanted to be more than just friends.

The reality is that this story was only the beginning for Praise Community Church. Little did we know that this very moment in time would prove to be the catalyst that would aid the church in moving through the most difficult time of its existence—the suicide of its previous pastor in May 2010. It would also be the single defining moment when the face of the church would be forever changed from the natural ways of man to the supernatural ways of God.

What was even more impressive to me, however, was not that the church began to move in supernatural ways of ministry, but that the people of Praise began to experience greater levels of intimacy within their relationship with God. The very person of the Holy Spirit came upon them and filled them. A union had taken place in a way they never experienced before. God became more real to them that evening than any other time previously. Something mysterious took place. God deposited even more of Himself within the present believers. The Creator and the created became more than friends. They were becoming "one flesh."

ENDNOTE

I.   Bill Johnson, *When Heaven Invades Earth* (Shippensburg, PA: Destiny Image, 2003).

Chapter 8

BECOMING ONE FLESH

*For this reason a man shall leave his father and his
mother, and be joined to his wife; and they shall
become one flesh* (Genesis 2:24).

The Great Mystery

Scripture reveals that it has always been God's plan for man
and woman to come together and become one flesh. Jesus Himself
answered the Pharisees' question if it was lawful for a man to divorce his wife for any reason at all in this way:

*And He answered and said, "Have you not read that He who created
them from the beginning made them male and female, and said, 'For
this reason a man shall leave his father and mother and be joined to
his wife, and the two shall become one flesh'? So they are no longer*

two, but one flesh. What therefore God has joined together, let no man separate" (Matthew 19:4-6).

Based on Jesus' response, the answer seems clear. Man was to leave his father and mother and be joined to his wife and become one flesh. Although there is much debate over what this idea of "becoming one flesh" represents, I will not pretend to know all the dynamics that comprise this great mystery. Paul, in his letter to the Ephesians, echoes this same sentiment by making this statement concerning the idea of becoming one flesh: *"This mystery is great"* (Eph. 5:32).

The amazing thing about Paul's comment is that it isn't only limited to the mystery of husband and wife becoming one flesh. In the context of Ephesians 5, Paul is also speaking to the mystery that is found in Christ's relationship to the Church. It is within this chapter that Paul mirrors the relationship between husband and wife to be like that of Christ's to the Church. A man is to love his wife in the same way that Christ loved the Church and gave Himself up for her (see Eph. 5:25). Wives are to be subject to their husbands just as the Church is subject to Christ (see Eph. 5:24).

As a result, I believe it is safe to assume that it is not only the husband and wife who are to become one flesh, but the Church and Christ as well. There is no greater evidence of this than what is found in the previous chapter—the Holy Spirit living inside the believer. I'm not sure it's possible to "become one" at any greater level than God Himself making His home within us.

In God's eyes, we are prime real estate.

But the question that each believer must ask him or herself is this: "Have I chosen to become one with Him?"

Union

Love by its nature seeks union.[1]

Thankfully, Christ revealed that the invitation into union with Him is not limited to the religious and the keepers of the law, but to the broken, the lost, and the suffering:

> But when Jesus heard this, He said, "It is not those who are healthy who need a physician, but those who are sick. But go and learn what this means: 'I desire compassion, and not sacrifice,' *for I did not come to call the righteous, but sinners*" (Matthew 9:12-13).

In his book, *The Furious Longing of God*, Brennan Manning quotes Jean Vanier as having said this about who Jesus invites to Himself:

> It is not reserved for those who are well-known mystics or for those who do wonderful things for the poor…. [It is for] those poor enough to welcome Jesus. It is for people living ordinary lives and who feel lonely. It is for all those who are old, hospitalized or out of work, who open their hearts in trust to Jesus and cry out for his healing love.[2]

There is no partiality with God (see Eph. 6:9). There is only love.

In his same book, Manning shares his revelation of how much God loves us. Through reading and praying over the words of John

17:22-23, Manning concludes that the degree of Abba's love for us is in direct proportion to His love for Jesus.[3] This truth is contained in the very words of Jesus found in John 15:9: *"Just as the Father has loved Me, I have also loved you; abide in My love."*

The act of abiding is an invitation that we find throughout the 15th chapter of John's Gospel. I will discuss the fruitful results of abiding in Christ in the next chapter. For now, I'd like to focus on the idea that we are invited to make our home in Him in the same way He's chosen to make His home in us. We are invited into union with our Creator—the same union that Jesus experienced with His Father.

> *No one has seen God at any time; the only begotten God **who is in the bosom of the Father**, He has explained Him* (John 1:18).

Even in the midst of this invitation to know Jesus in the same way He knew His Father, He remains a gentleman:

> *Behold, **I stand at the door and knock**; if anyone hears My voice and opens the door, I will come in to him and will dine with him, and he with Me* (Revelation 3:20).

We know God's desire when it comes to His end of the relationship with us. His love toward us isn't a mystery. His desire for intimacy cries out through the blood of Jesus. And yet He leaves the decision to us. *He's standing at the door and knocking.* Do we continue to remain where we are in our relationship with Him or do we open up the doors of our heart to a greater intimacy? In the same way that the man asks permission to marry the love of his life from her father, Jesus is asking our permission to go deeper with Him.

I'm convinced that as we grow in our knowledge of Him (who He is and how He feels about us), we will rip the doors open with eagerness.

Positioned to Receive

Here's the reality: When I know Him, I am more than willing to give myself entirely to Him. There's no risk involved. When my spirit catches up to the revelation that He is for me and not against me (see Rom. 8:31), I am willing to cannonball into the rivers of His grace and love. I don't have to dip my toe in the water and test it.

When I know Him, He becomes my heart's desire.

When I know Him, I want nothing more than to spend every moment of my life in His presence, which He is more than willing to pour out.

The entire book up to this point has been shaped to help answer Paul's prayer for the Ephesian church (and what I believe to be a necessary prayer for all believers):

> *For this reason I too, having heard of the faith in the Lord Jesus which exists among you and your love for all the saints, do not cease giving thanks for you, while making mention of you in my prayers; that the God of our Lord Jesus Christ, the Father of glory, **may give to you a spirit of wisdom and of revelation in the knowledge of Him*** (Ephesians 1:15-17).

Like I mentioned before in a previous chapter—*knowing is everything*. We come to know Him through His Word. We come to know Him through prayer. We come to know Him through worship. More than anything, we come to know Him through encounter. May your reading of His Word and seeking Him in prayer and experiencing Him in worship lead you into an encounter. Bill Johnson, senior pastor of Bethel Church in Redding, California and renowned author, says that if these disciplines do not lead us into an encounter, they only serve to make us more religious through the acquiring of knowledge about Him rather than knowing Him through relationship.

Although I cannot force you to make the decision to deepen your relationship with God, I do pray that there has been a deposit of spiritual salt placed in your mouth that has resulted in a thirst for more of Him.

The next time you pray, meditate on His love for you. Meditate on what you've learned up to this point. Pray from the perspective that you are His desire. Pray from a position of rest. He's done all the work. He's been the one pursuing you. He is the male in this relationship. Will you open the door? Will you go deeper than ever before?

There is a calling out.
Can you hear the sound? Can you hear His voice?
He's simply saying, "Come up here.
Come up here, My beloved, My bride."[4]

Endnotes

1. Brennan Manning, *The Furious Longing of God* (Ontario, Canada: David C. Cook, 2009), 59.

2. Jean Vanier, *Drawn Into the Mystery of God Through the Gospel of John* (Mahwah, NJ: Paulist Press, 2004), 296.

3. Manning, *The Furious Longing of God*, 61.

4. Lyrics from the song "The Invitation" by Nic and Rachael Billman from the album *The Invitation.*

PART III

Come Up Here, My Beloved, My Bride

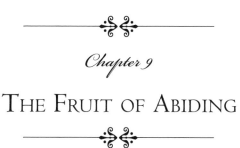

Chapter 9

THE FRUIT OF ABIDING

I am the vine, you are the branches; he who abides
*in Me and I in him, he bears much fruit, **for apart***
from Me you can do nothing (John 15:5).

Fruit

For three years of my life, I had lived in the small town of Wilmore, Kentucky while I was a student at Asbury Theological Seminary. The years 2002 to 2005 exposed me to some of the greatest theological training of my life. One of my favorite professors at Asbury was a man by the name of Dr. Steve Seamands. He had taught my Basic Christian Doctrine class.

Seamands, whose family has a rich heritage at Asbury, taught something in class one day that has truly helped to shape my relationship with God. (It still affects it to this very day!) What's so amazing is that this truth wasn't revealed through regular class hours. The revelation wasn't deposited during "class time." Instead, it was shared five minutes before the start of class during our "devotion time."

You see, at Asbury, the majority of classes begin with a brief sharing of the Word along with some commentary or prayer from the professors. On one particular day in the fall of 2003, Dr. Seamands read this passage to my class:

> *I am the true vine, and My Father is the vinedresser. Every branch in Me that does not bear fruit, He takes away; and every branch that bears fruit, He prunes it so that it may bear more fruit. You are already clean because of the word which I have spoken to you. **Abide in Me**, and I in you. As the branch cannot bear fruit of itself unless it abides in the vine, so neither can you unless you **abide in Me**. I am the vine, you are the branches; he who **abides in Me** and I in him, he bears much fruit, for apart from Me you can do nothing. If anyone does not **abide in Me**, he is thrown away as a branch and dries up; and they gather them, and cast them into the fire and they are burned. If you **abide in Me**, and My words abide in you, ask whatever you wish, and it will be done for you. My Father is glorified by this, that you bear much fruit, and so prove to be My disciples. Just as the Father has loved Me, I have also loved you; **abide in My love*** (John 15:1-9).

It shouldn't take anyone very long to notice the pattern that is being birthed through Jesus' words in this passage. The pattern, like I've been saying all along, is an invitation. It's an invitation to rest in, make your home in, get lost in, and remain in the love of God.

Dr. Seamands explained to the class that this is all that God requires of us—to abide.

It made so much sense. It was so simple. Everything flows out of this abiding. There truly is a necessity to this thing called intimacy. All that we have and are able to do is because of His grace. It's not enough for us to bite our lip and try to "be a better Christian." Although we do work out our salvation with fear and trembling, we must never forget that it's He who is at work in us both to will and to work for His good pleasure (see Phil. 2:12-13). It's His work of grace and our yielding to it that results in our becoming like Him.

The one phrase that jumps out at me more than the rest from John's passage is this one: *"...for apart from Me you can do nothing."* The *nothing* that Jesus was referring to was the fruit of the abiding process. Jesus refers to Himself as the *true vine* and us as *the branches*. In the same way that the branches cannot live or bear fruit apart from their life source, the vine, neither can we apart from our life source, Jesus.

We were never meant to be disconnected or separated from the Giver of life. We were always meant to bear much fruit.

Interestingly, the fruit that Jesus was referring to is not the fruit of the Spirit that Paul wrote about in Galatians 5:22-23. Contextually, the fruit that Jesus was speaking of is found in John 14:12.

> *Truly, truly, I say to you, he who believes in Me,* **the works that I do***, he will do also; and* **greater works** *than these he will do; because I go to the Father* (John 14:12).

The fruit is the works of Jesus and the greater works. The fruit of abiding is the supernatural lifestyle that's available to the believer because Jesus had gone to the Father in order that He might send the Helper, the Holy Spirit. And it is this lifestyle—the lifestyle that bears much fruit—that glorifies God and proves that we are His disciples (see John 15:8).

Faith

Prior to my sitting down to write this book, God showed me that it was the friends of God—those intimately connected to Him—who made the most impact in human history. It was those who abided in His presence and believed that He did all things well (see Mark 7:37). They tasted and saw that He was good (see Ps. 34:8). They trusted in Him. They had faith in His faithfulness and His love.

Hebrews says this:

> *And without faith it is impossible to please Him, for he who comes to God **must believe that He is** and that He is a rewarder of those who seek Him* (Hebrews 11:6).

Believe that He is what? First and foremost, that He exists. How could we come to Him if we weren't able to at least recognize the very foundation by which we come? Indeed, we wouldn't approach Him if we didn't believe He existed. We wouldn't even pray.

Secondly, we must believe that He is good. This is why the above verse ends with the charge that *"He is a rewarder of those who seek Him."* Only He who is good would reward such faith. But in order to believe that He is good, there must have been an *encounter* with His goodness. There must have been some kind of experience by which His faithfulness was sampled and tasted. This is the process by which we come to have faith—we encounter His goodness, mercy, love, and faithfulness, and faith is born. Every subsequent experience with these attributes serves to increase our faith. It is on these premises that I believe that the pillars of faith found in Hebrews 11 were able to do what they did.

Whenever we read that all-familiar phrase, *by faith*, found in Hebrews 11, we come to understand that these great men and women, these "clouds of witnesses" (see Heb. 12:1), did what they did through faith in God's goodness and faithfulness. Their faith had an origin. Their faith had an anchor. It was deeply rooted in their encounters with God that enabled them to experience this God of infinite power and love. For this reason, the writer of Hebrews says that these men and women of God championed the following things through their faith:

> *...conquered kingdoms, performed acts of righteousness, obtained promises, shut the mouths of lions, quenched the power of fire, escaped the edge of the sword, from weakness were made strong, became mighty in war, put foreign armies to flight. Women received back their dead by resurrection; and others were tortured, not accepting their release, so that they might obtain a better resurrection; and others experienced mockings and scourgings, yes, also chains and imprisonment. They were stoned, they were sawn in two, they were tempted, they were put to death with the sword; they went about in sheepskins, in goatskins, being destitute, afflicted, ill-treated (men of whom the world was not worthy), wandering in deserts and mountains and caves and holes in the ground* (Hebrews 11:33-38).

No one is able to do or endure such things except by faith and faith alone. And this faith must be rooted in the goodness and faithfulness of God. Otherwise, these men and women of the faith wouldn't have performed these mighty acts if their faith was rooted in any other thing.

If it's true that such faith is born out of encounters with God's attributes, then faith is also a fruit of abiding in Christ. When we abide in Him, we encounter Him. We rest in His love for us, and in the process we come to know Him in an even greater way, which leads to the continual growth of our faith—a faith that can accomplish the very things we read about in Hebrews 11 and more.

Answers to Prayer and Becoming More Like Him

Jesus said, *"If you abide in Me, and My words abide in you, ask whatever you wish, and it will be done for you"* (John 15:7). Please understand that this isn't some formula or method by which you can get whatever you want. You don't wake up and say, "I wonder how I can work this Gospel so I can fulfill every one of my selfish desires." I don't think that is what Jesus had in mind through the above verse.

What happens in abiding, however, is this: I find that His desires become my desires. I believe that this is what Jesus is referring to when He says, *"If you abide in Me, **and My words abide in you.**"* If His words abide in me, the sperma of God or the seed of His Word has been planted within my heart. If nurtured correctly, these very words will result in the birth of the likeness of His heart within me. As a result, rather than praying from the position of selfishness, I find myself praying out of His heart that has been placed within me. When I pray from this place, I find that He can't help but to want to answer my prayers.

It's very difficult to not be influenced by someone after you've spent a significant amount of time in their presence. After a while, you may even begin to take on traits or characteristics of that person. I believe this is what happens when we abide in Christ.

In the same way that the skin of Moses' face had shone after speaking with God on Mount Sinai (see Exod. 34:29-30), I believe that there are deposits of God placed within us as we abide in His presence. We know this to be true because of the following verses:

> *But if the ministry of death, in letters engraved on stones, came with glory, so that the sons of Israel could not look intently at the face of Moses because of the glory of his face, fading as it was, how will the ministry of the Spirit fail to be even more with glory?* (2 Corinthians 3:7-8)

Could it be since we find ourselves to be living in the time of the ministry of the Spirit that every time we abide in His presence we leave looking more like Him than when we came?

Yes. I believe we do.

I do not think it is possible for people to come into the presence of God without something within them or about them dying and becoming more like Him. I believe this is indeed the process of *"being transformed into the same image from glory to glory, just as from the Lord, the Spirit"* (2 Cor. 3:18). And I believe that one of the ways that we experience this process is through prayer.

Chapter 10

INTIMACY THROUGH PRAYER

May my prayer be counted as incense before You; the lifting up of my hands as the evening offering (Psalm 141:2).

When you pray, you are not to be like the hypocrites; for they love to stand and pray in the synagogues and on the street corners so that they may be seen by men. Truly I say to you, they have their reward in full. But you, when you pray, go into your inner room, close your door and pray to your Father who is in secret, and your Father who sees what is done in secret will reward you (Matthew 6:5-6).

I'm Not Crazy!

My wife, Nicole, is currently reading Beni Johnson's book, *The Happy Intercessor*. In her book, Beni provides some insights that have further helped me in understanding myself and my never-ending quest for wanting to know God and to have more of Him. It's quite simple, really. I'm the type of mystic that Beni refers to as a "cave dweller."

According to Beni:

> Mystics are people who live in right relationship with God and who have truly surrendered themselves to knowing Him more, no matter what the cost. Mystics do not seek after fame, glory, or worldly desires, but they have chosen instead to lay their entire lives down so that they can hear the heartbeat of Heaven. Mystics are people who have a continual awareness of God.

> Mystics are not satisfied with what is in front of them. They want to see more. Mystics see beyond this reality and into the spirit realm.

> To them, God is more real than life. God is their life. Mystics see how the spirit realm connects with the worldly realms. In other words, they see how and where Heaven is invading earth. They take all of those connections, and they put them together and make sense of it all. Mystics are able to see into the spiritual realm and use it to help define what is going on in the earthly realm. In this sense, they help to bring Heaven to earth.

> To the mystic, the spirit realm is a safe place. To them, the spiritual realm can often seem more real than the earthly realm. In fact, a mystic thrives on experiencing that heavenly realm.[1]

Although I do not think that all Beni describes above is true of me, I do think these following words of hers help:

> To me, the mystics are just normal people. They are normal people who are consumed by the presence of God. They are normal people who enjoy being with God and who know how to move in and out of the secret place.[2]

Beni also helps me to understand why I am the way I am by narrowing the focus even more by describing specific types of mystics. One of the types of mystics she describes is that which I labeled myself at the beginning of this chapter—a "cave dweller." Beni describes cave dwellers this way:

> A cave dweller likes to be alone with God and would spend all of his time alone with God if he could.[3]

My wife would tell you very pointedly that Beni's words describe me perfectly. I am the type of person, or shall we say mystic, who loves to be alone with God and would spend all my time alone with Him if I could. I'm consumed by His presence. And I know how to move in and out of the secret place. All of this time I thought that I was strange for wanting to spend as much time with God as I could. It turns out that I'm not crazy after all! I'm actually normal. Thanks for clearing that up for not only me but my wife also, Beni!

The Reward of His Presence

Although there are various ways by which people encounter God and experience His presence, prayer is the vehicle through which I encounter and experience Him the quickest. In her book, *No Greater Love*, Mother Theresa says that:

Real prayer is union with God, a union as vital as that of the vine to the branch, which is the illustration Jesus gives us in the Gospel of John. We need prayer.... Prayer is the very life of oneness, of being one with Christ. Therefore, prayer is as necessary as the air, as the blood in our body, as anything, to keep us alive to the grace of God.[4]

Indeed, it is in my secret place, my prayer closet, that our intimacy together soars to greater heights. Truly, there's no other place I'd rather be. It's here that I taste of His goodness and He overwhelms me with His presence.

When I retreat to be alone with God, I find that I commonly do two things to access His presence:

1. I focus on Him, and

2. I listen to worship music.

What I mean when I say "focus on Him" is this: I focus on His love for me and what I know about Him. Mother Theresa says it beautifully:

Often a deep and fervent look at Christ is the best prayer: I look at Him and He looks at me.[5]

When I know who He is, I can engage Him and recognize His presence faster than normal. Most of the time, I simply lie face down on the floor and just think about Him. Other times, I'll sit on the floor and prop myself up against the wall. It's in my knowing of who He is that I'm able to practice both the disciplines of *stillness* and *silence*.

"Be still, and know that I am God..." (Ps. 46:10 NIV). When you know Him, there's no striving in prayer, only rest. I rest in the fact that He is the provider of every good and perfect gift (see James 1:17). I rest in the fact that nothing can separate me from His love (see Rom. 8:38-39). My Father is a big God!

Atmosphere is also important for me when it comes to meeting with God. As a cave dweller, I naturally like to be alone when it comes to being with Him. Not everyone is wired this way, however. I also enjoy having minimal lighting. There's something about creating an environment through which I experience an intimate connection with Him at a more rapid rate. It's beautiful.

Worship music is also a key element in my ability to encounter God. I am deeply in love with spontaneous forms of worship. I also find that in the same way the Spirit intercedes for me with groaning too deep for words (see Rom. 8:26), I find that worship music can often express what I am feeling inside. Sometimes I don't even have to pray. I'll just listen to what is being spoken through song and my spirit will agree with it.

In Matthew 6:5-6, Jesus warns those whom are gathered to hear the famous "Sermon on the Mount" to not pray in such a way that would draw attention to yourself. If this is your sole motive, you will have your reward, Jesus says. You will get the attention you are looking for! But if you pray in secret, you will receive a different reward— the reward of His presence. It's during this time of praying in secret where we meet face to face and I get completely lost in Him. It's in those moments of praying alone that I talk to Him and He talks to me. It's here where I feel His love for me. But the most beautiful thing of all is this: When I am finished communing with Him through prayer, I look more like Him than when we began, because the reality is that no man can see His face and live (see Exod. 33:20).

Every time I pray, I know something within me dies. Whenever the Jews would worship God, they'd take something along that wasn't leaving with them—an animal for sacrifice or grain for a burnt offering. This is the mentality I bring into my alone time with God. I know that something within me is going to be left behind. I'm truly moving from glory to glory.

Because I find that more of me dies in the presence of God, I find the stunning reality that I'm able to contain more of Him. Mother Theresa explains this phenomenon better than I could by saying:

> Love to pray. Feel the need to pray often during the day. Prayer enlarges the heart until it is capable of containing God's gift of Himself. Ask and seek and your heart will grow big enough to receive Him and keep Him as your own.[6]

I find these words to be both absolutely captivating and true. Prayer enlarges the heart. Why? Because the very act of prayer requires humility. I come knowing that I need His presence. I come confessing that I'm in desperate need of Him. It is in humility that the very words of John the Baptist ring true: *"He must increase, but I must decrease"* (John 3:30). In prayer, He increases and I decrease. And when I decrease, He fills me with Himself. Beni Johnson echoes this idea by stating:

> When I spend time in the secret place, alone with God, I become so wrapped up in His presence that every other desire loses its importance to me. When I allow His presence to consume me, I surrender myself

so completely to His will that my desires begin to line up with His. I become fully engulfed in His presence, lost in a sea of His beauty, and captivated by His love. In that place is the fullness of joy, the fullness of peace, the fullness of love, and the fullness of acceptance. In that place, I become one with Him.

The reward is His presence and becoming one with Him…and there's no greater reward I could ask for.[7]

Take My Word for It

My challenge to you, the reader, is to stop doing what you're doing right now and get alone with Him. Put the book down if you have to. When you get alone, I want you to keep these things in mind:

- He loves you. He really, really loves you (see John 15:9).

- He wants to spend time with you more than you could possibly imagine (see John 15).

- He wants to talk to you and you can hear His voice (see John 10:27).

- He sings over you and exults with joy over you (see Zeph. 3:17).

- You're worth the blood of Jesus.

In fact, as you go and find your quiet place, the only thing I want you to pray is this: "Father, thank You for loving me." If you keep praying those words even in spite of circumstances that tell you otherwise, I promise that you will experience His presence. I promise that you will feel His love wash over you.

ENDNOTES

1. Beni Johnson, *The Happy Intercessor* (Shippensburg, PA: Destiny Image, 2009), 164.

2. Ibid, 166-167.

3. Ibid, 165.

4. Mother Theresa, *No Greater Love* (Novato, CA: New World Library, 2001), 11-14.

5. Ibid, 7.

6. Ibid, 4.

7. Johnson, *The Happy Intercessor,* 169.

Chapter 11

COME TO ME

*Now on the last day, the great day of the feast, Jesus
stood and cried out, saying, "If anyone is thirsty, let
him **come to Me** and drink. He who believes in Me,
as the Scripture said, 'From his innermost being
will flow rivers of **living water**.'" But this He spoke
of the Spirit, whom those who believed in Him were
to receive; for the Spirit was not yet given, because
Jesus was not yet glorified (John 7:37-39).*

How Thirsty Are You?

A few years ago, the Lord revealed to me the name of my itinerant ministry. He said that it will be called "Living Waters." Although
my itinerant ministry is in its budding years, I remain patient and

yet wait anxiously for the time when the Lord will have me traveling full-time, speaking to people about His great love and demonstrating it through the power of the Spirit. It is truly my desire to echo the words and lifestyle of Paul:

> *And when I came to you, brethren, I did not come with superiority of speech or of wisdom, proclaiming to you the testimony of God. For I determined to know nothing among you except Jesus Christ, and Him crucified. I was with you in weakness and in fear and in much trembling, and my message and my preaching were not in persuasive words of wisdom, but in demonstration of the Spirit and of power, so that your faith would not rest on the wisdom of men, but on the power of God* (I Corinthians 2:1-5).

It is my hope and prayer that through this book, you will take the invitation of Jesus quite seriously:

> *...If anyone is thirsty, let him come to Me and drink. He who believes in Me, as the Scripture said, "From his innermost being will flow rivers of living water"* (John 7:37-38).

These rivers of living water represent the actual dwelling of God within the believer in the person of the Holy Spirit. The implication is that it's the Holy Spirit who quenches thirst. The invitation is to drink from His rivers and to know Him in an even more intimate way.

This invitation never ceases. God never grows tired of pursuing you. In the words of Heidi Baker, founder of Iris Ministries, "Because Jesus died, there is always enough."

So the question that needs to be answered is this: How thirsty are you?

The next question that should be answered is this one: If you are still thirsty in an unsatisfied way in your relationship with God, where are you drinking from?

A Conversation About Water

The story contained in John 4:1-26 is a great commentary on the previously posed questions and is an appropriate way to sum up all that this book has discussed up to this point. I'm sure many of you know this story. It's the story of Jesus and the woman at the well (i.e. the Woman of Samaria). Like the parable of the prodigal son, let's examine this story in detail as well.

Jesus had left Judea and was heading to Galilee, but He needed to pass through Samaria to reach the end of His destination. Tired from His journey, Jesus decided to pull up a seat next to Jacob's Well. While Jesus was reclining and recovering from the demands of His trip, there came a woman from Samaria to draw water from the very well that became Jesus' rest stop.

Catching this woman completely off guard, Jesus said to her, *"Give Me a drink"* (John 4:7). The reason for this woman's sudden surprise at Jesus' comment is found in the fact that Jews had very little contact, if any at all, with Samaritans. This is why this woman asked the following question of Jesus: *"How is it that You, being a Jew, ask me for a drink since I am a Samaritan woman?"* (John 4:9).

If it wasn't startling enough for Jesus, being a Jew, to engage this Samaritan woman in conversation, He goes on to drop this bomb:

> *If you knew the gift of God, and who it is who says to you, "Give Me a drink," you would have asked Him, and He would have given you living water* (John 4:10).

Based on what we already know about Jesus and how He conducts Himself, we know that He isn't talking about H$_2$O. But His very comment draws this woman deeper into conversation with Him, and it would be this very conversation that would eventually transform an entire city. What started out as a conversation about water quickly became the bait on Jesus' hook to lead this woman into an encounter with the very One she knew was to come—the Messiah.

The next few interchanges in conversation between Jesus and this woman are absolutely fascinating. It's here that I'd like to spend most of my time connecting the dots of this book and bringing the sum of it all to a close.

The Well Is Deep

After Jesus makes the comment that He would have given this woman living water had she realized who He was and asked Him, the woman observes the lunacy behind His statement when she notices that He has no bucket to draw any water with. Let's take a look at the rest of their dialogue together:

> She said to Him, "Sir, You have nothing to draw with and **the well is deep**; where then do You get that living water? You are not greater than our father Jacob, are You, who gave us the well, and drank of it himself and his sons and his cattle?" Jesus answered and said to her, "Everyone who drinks of this water will thirst again; but whoever drinks of the water that I will give him shall never thirst; but the water that I will give him will become in him a well of water springing up to eternal life." The woman said to Him, "Sir, give me this water, so I will not be thirsty nor come all the way here to draw." He said

*to her, "Go, call your husband and come here." The woman answered and said, "I have no husband." Jesus said to her, "You have correctly said, 'I have no husband'; **for you have had five husbands, and the one whom you now have is not your husband**; this you have said truly"* (John 4:11-18).

The well is deep is a string of words that has always caught my attention, and it is within these words that the deeper revelation of this story is contained.

The reason why the physical well that Jesus is reclining against is deep is because the contents that fill the well itself are shallow. Make no mistake, the water within the well isn't deep, it's the distance between the top of the well to the actual water itself that results in the lengthy gap.

In the same way that the physical well was deep because its contents were shallow, the well of the woman's soul was deep because that which was filling her was shallow—her previous five husbands and the man she currently found herself with.

The water that the woman from Samaria was drinking from was men, plain and simple. Jesus was aware of this and He called her out on it. But He didn't leave her stuck in her thirst; rather, He provided the way to quench it:

But whoever drinks of the water that I will give him shall never thirst; but the water that I will give him will become in him a well of water springing up to eternal life (John 4:14).

What Will Your Decision Be?

The truth is many people are drinking from wells that do not spring up to eternal life—including Christians. If we were truly drinking from the rivers of living water, *we wouldn't do the things we do.* Men. Women. Drugs. Alcohol. Money. Possessions. Success. Religion. It's all the same. They are all methods by which people either medicate themselves or seek to find significance or, worse yet, love.

Significance and love can only be found in one place—Jesus Christ.

On the last, great day of the Feast of Booths, Jesus *stood up* and *cried out, "If anyone is thirsty, let him come to Me and drink"* (John 7:37). It is this statement and this statement alone that best conveys the intensity of Jesus' invitation to us to dive even deeper into our relationship with Him. Why? Because when rabbis taught the people, they did so sitting down. In this particular verse, however, we find Jesus once again breaking the mold. He stood up. He not only stood up, He cried out.

He stood to get everyone's attention. He cried out so that all of the world may hear and so this invitation would forever ring in the depths of our heart. Jesus also says this in the Book of Revelation:

> *...I will give to the one who thirsts from the spring of the water of life without cost* (Revelation 21:6).

The invitation is open. This is not an exclusive club. The condition for admittance is simple—thirst.

"Come to Me and drink."

The argument has been made. You are worth the blood of Jesus. There isn't a single thing He wouldn't do to have you. You are the object of His desire. Will He be yours?

If you want more of God, if you want to come to the waters and begin to encounter God in ways you've maybe only read about or dreamed of, I encourage you to pray this prayer:

Father, I hunger and thirst for You. I want nothing more than to encounter You right now. I pray that You would come and meet me right where I am. I give You full permission to overtake me. I give You full permission to overwhelm me. I know there's more and I want to experience You to the fullest. Whatever might be standing in the way of You and I going deeper, I pray that You would remove it. You're all that I want.

Jesus, I pray to know Your love in an even greater measure. Come and baptize me with the Holy Spirit and with fire.

Holy Spirit, come and fill me. I pray that You would manifest Yourself to me in the same way You did to those in Acts 2 on the day of Pentecost. Fill me with Your power and increase the measure of Your presence within me.

Thank You, Father, for loving me and for answering these prayers. In the name of Jesus Christ I pray and ask all these things. Amen.

Afterthought

An Invitation from Steven Curtis Chapman

Dive

The long-awaited rains have fallen hard upon the thirsty ground
Have carved their way to where the wild and rushing river can be found.
And like the rains I have been carried here to where the river flows, yeah,
My heart is racin' and my knees are weak as I walk to the edge.
I know there is no turning back once my feet have left the ledge,
And in the rush I hear a voice, it's telling me it's time to
Take the leap of faith,
So here I go.

I'm diving in,
I'm going deep,
In over my head I wanna be

Caught in the rush,
Lost in the flow,
In over my head I wanna go.
The river's deep,
The river's wide,
The river's water is alive.
So sink or swim,
I'm diving in,
I'm diving in.

There is a supernatural power in this mighty river's flow.
It can bring the dead to life, and it can fill an empty soul
And give a heart the only thing worth livin' and worth dyin' for, yeah.
But we will never know the awesome power of the grace of God
Until we let ourselves get swept away into this holy flood.
So if you'll take my hand, we'll close our eyes and count to three,
And take the leap of faith
Come on let's go.[1]

ENDNOTE

1. Lyrics from the song "Dive" by Steven Curtis Chapman, from the album *Speechless*.

ABOUT BRIAN CONNOLLY

Brian Connolly serves as Pastor of Evangelism at Praise Community Church in York, PA, where he was used by God to usher in the anointing through the baptism of the Holy Spirit. It was during this time when the Holy Spirit fell on the 120-plus people assembled to receive more of God. As a result, Praise Community Church is now Kingdom focused with a Kingdom message.

Brian is happily married to his wife of seven years, Nicole, and is the proud father of his beautiful three-year-old daughter, Emma. He is also a graduate of Asbury Theological Seminary.

Currently, God has been using Brian's budding itinerant ministry to awaken His Church to the reality that we must press into His love in order that *we* might love. Indeed, God so desperately wants us to become more than we are with Him. He wants us to become "one flesh." It's in Him that we move, that we exist, and that we have our being (see Acts 17:28). It's the love of the Father that sets captives free and binds up the broken heart.

IN THE RIGHT HANDS, THIS BOOK WILL CHANGE LIVES!

Most of the people who need this message will not be looking for this book. To change their lives, you need to put a copy of this book in their hands.

> *But others (seeds) fell into good ground, and brought forth fruit, some a hundred-fold, some sixty-fold, some thirty-fold* (Matthew 13:8).

Our ministry is constantly seeking methods to find the good ground, the people who need this anointed message to change their lives. Will you help us reach these people?

> *Remember this—a farmer who plants only a few seeds will get a small crop. But the one who plants generously will get a generous crop* (2 Corinthians 9:6).

EXTEND THIS MINISTRY BY SOWING 3 BOOKS, 5 BOOKS, 10 BOOKS, OR MORE TODAY, AND BECOME A LIFE CHANGER!

Thank you,

Don Nori Sr., Founder
Destiny Image
Since 1982